UTOPIA a commonwealth. Sir Thomas More coined the name from Greek words meaning "no place," in recognition of the fact that no ideal society actually exists; and ~~the point of the book lies in the ironic contrast between Utopia and More's own society.~~ Written originally in Latin (1516) for scholars, UTOPIA was not translated into English until 1551. The book has since had a universal effect on the course of political theory and the adjective *utopian* has become an accepted abstract term of almost every modern language.

The translator, Peter K. Marshall, M.A. (Oxon.), is an Assistant Professor of the Classics, Amherst College. He previously was Assistant Lecturer in Latin and Greek at the University of Liverpool and has held fellowships at the Universities of Oxford and Liverpool.

The author of the Introduction, John Anthony Scott, presently Chairman of the Department of History, Fieldston School, Riverdale, New York, is a distinguished American historian and teacher. He holds a B.A. and M.A. from Oxford University, a M.A. and Ph.D. from Columbia University, and has been a member of the History Faculty of Amherst College. His published articles and books cover a broad range of historical subjects of both popular and scholarly interest.

UTOPIA
Sir Thomas More

Translated by Peter K. Marshall
Introduction by John Anthony Scott

WASHINGTON SQUARE PRESS
PUBLISHED BY POCKET BOOKS NEW YORK

Utopia was first printed in Latin by Theodore Martin at Louvain, under the editorship of Erasmus, Ægidius, Paludanus, and other of More's friends in Flanders, towards the end of 1516.

A Washington Square Press Publication of
POCKET BOOKS, a division of Simon & Schuster, Inc.
1230 Avenue of the Americas, New York, N.Y. 10020

ISBN: 0-671-66429-8

First Pocket Books printing April 1965

27 26 25 24 23 22 21 20 19 18

WASHINGTON SQUARE PRESS and WSP colophon are
registered trademarks of Simon & Schuster, Inc.

Printed in the U.S.A.

INTRODUCTION

THOMAS MORE was born in London, England, in 1478, the son of John More, a prosperous lawyer and judge. More, who was to become a fluent Latinist, received his grounding in Latin at St. Anthony's school in London, and then, while still not more than twelve years old, was sent to live in the household of John Morton, Archbishop of Canterbury and Lord Chancellor of the realm. Here the child stayed for two years, learning the manners appropriate to a gentleman. The episode would be vividly re-created in the famous dialogue between Raphael Hythloday and the members of the Chancellor's entourage which appears in the first book of *Utopia*.

Following this experience, the fourteen-year-old boy was sent to Oxford—probably to Christ Church—and after two years there was transferred by his father to the Inns of Court to be trained in the profession of the law. More possessed the makings of a brilliant lawyer, but he had no love for the profession imposed upon him, and he followed the paternal footsteps with reluctance. Soon after his return to London—in 1499 to be precise—he made the acquaintance of Erasmus, then on the first of several visits to England. He entered into that close association with the Humanist movement that was to prove of decisive importance for his life and work.

The movement of European thought and letters that

we call Humanism found, during the Renaissance, its greatest exponent in the person of Desiderius Erasmus. Its greatest English practitioners during the early sixteenth century were John Colet, dean of St. Paul's, William Grocyn, vicar of St. Lawrence Jewry, William Lily, first High Master of St. Paul's School, Thomas Linacre, a founder of the Royal College of Physicians, and Thomas More himself. The Humanist movement, in the person of men such as these, scored great achievements during the first twenty years of the sixteenth century.

We may characterize Humanism as a many-sided literary, scientific and ideological movement that was to exert an enduring influence on Western thought and culture and that was to establish the basis for our modern social sciences. Humanist scholarship was concerned, first and foremost, to recover the ancient texts that provided the historical underpinnings of Western religion, philosophy and science. Since the heritage of the ancient world had to be recovered from Greek, Hebrew and Latin texts, the Humanists naturally placed great emphasis on the mastery of these tongues. They placed an especial stress upon the recovery of Greek as the lost language of both science and religion, and in general upon winning direct access to the Greek heritage through firsthand study of the old texts and through new translations of them. The motivation of Humanist scholarship was here eminently scientific—the recovery of the original historical evidence and the casting aside of the second-hand accounts, commentaries and glosses which over the centuries had become substitutes for the study of the original sources of European thought and culture. Humanism sought out these original sources, began to study them with impassioned zeal and concerned itself with the formation of fresh and independent conclusions about them. This scholarly impulse has had an enduring impact upon Western intellectual life; its effects have not yet exhausted themselves, even in the course of four centuries.

Humanist methods of scholarship were inescapably critical. Humanists, that is to say, were concerned with a critical assessment of original evidence, an estimate as to its authenticity and a discriminating conclusion as to its inner meaning. Many of the ancient sources, of course, antedated Christian revelation; they provided the critical mind with entirely fresh materials for the fashioning of a world outlook. This outlook remained, of course, fundamentally Christian, for the nature of Christian belief and the origins of Christianity were profoundly illuminated as a result of Humanist scholarship; but it was characterized by a fresh, bold and sweeping view of life antithetical to the methods and preoccupations of the medieval schools. Humanism contributed greatly to a new approach to the study of Christian religion and helped engineer major changes in man's concept of nature, of the world and of himself.

The Humanists came upon the scene at a critical time in the history of Western Europe. Medieval society was in decadence. Feudal kings—the Tudors in England, the Valois in France, the Hapsburgs in Spain and Germany —were engaged in chronic, bloody and dynastic struggles that drained their lands of treasure and exhausted their peoples. The luxury of the Church, the cynicism and profligacy of the nobility, both lay and ecclesiastical, the parasitism and corruption of the priesthood, had grown into a crying scandal. And to the evils of the old, dying order were added new evils stemming from the age of exploration and the appearance, among merchants and townsmen, of the profit motive as the mainspring of life and conduct. The lust for gold came brazenly forward to compete with the age-old lusts for land and glory as a dominant social ideal. But the masses of the people continued to live under cruel and beggarly conditions. Society to a sensitive observer presented shocking contrasts between the driving greed and luxury of the rich and the misery and oppression of the poor.

The Humanist movement—and this was the secret of its vitality—proceeded from an acute awareness of the actual conditions of life prevailing in Western Europe. Its central concern was a realistic appraisal of these conditions and the setting forth of a program for social and political reform. As the name implies, the central reason for Humanist activity was a passionate concern with the human condition, a passionate dedication to the improvement of human life and to the emancipation of man. Humanists—or at least the ones that we have named—were deeply religious men. Their scholarship received a sense of urgency and a social sanction from a deeply felt wish to bring about on earth that brotherly equality and that true understanding of the teaching of Jesus without which man, beset as he was by ignorance, evil laws, temptation and oppression, could not find his way to salvation. At the dawn of the modern world, social science made its appearance in England not as the desiccated discipline of pedants seeking knowledge for its own sake but as an instrumentality for the elevation and emancipation of mankind, for the eradication of cruelty, exploitation and illiteracy.

The Humanists examined the great social problems of their day realistically; not the least of their contributions was their bold and merciless castigation and exposure of folly, wickedness and vice. They denounced war as the greatest of evils; they proclaimed that the irresponsible and unbridled rule of kings was tyranny; they asserted the principle that a monarch's main concern ought to be the welfare of his subjects. They castigated the parasitism of the idle rich and they called for a far-reaching reform of the social order. *Utopia* was perhaps the greatest of the Humanists' many reform tracts. We shall find in it a detailed and specific program for the regeneration of society and the instrumentalities of government.

For a further elaboration of this interesting topic, the reader may, therefore, be referred to *Utopia* itself. But before passing on, a special word must be said about the Humanists' theory of the role of education in human affairs, and their special contribution to this subject. Their approach to education was, as in so much of their work, bold and pioneering. It was not enough, said they, that scholars should master Hebrew or Greek, edit and republish the ancient texts, and translate them. They must also teach; and teaching to them involved primarily the Greek and Roman classics. These must be taught, not so much for their own sakes, beautiful as they were, but because of the knowledge they transmitted, the inspiration that they imparted, and the excellence of the discipline that they afforded in the arts of thought, debate and self-expression. In England Dean Colet's great contribution to educational practice and his lasting monument to Humanist philosophy was the foundation of St. Paul's School in 1509. There 153 scholars would be taught

Latin and Greek and would receive a foundation in ancient science and philosophy.[1]

Thomas More, Dean Colet's close friend, was no schoolmaster, but he gave expression both in his own writings and in the education of his family to a well-defined educational philosophy. Educational theory is faced, at the start of its investigations, with the necessity to form an estimate of the capacities of man and the goals, therefore, that the education of these capacities must set itself. Such an estimate, of course, must relate to girls as well as to boys: the touchstone by which any educational theory may be measured is its approach to woman, to her intellectual and spiritual capacities, to her educability. Here More's contribution was a significant one. He proclaimed the equality of the sexes, at least insofar as education was concerned, in a society where woman was allotted a subordinate role. His convictions found expression in the strict training in *litterae humaniores* which he gave to his four children, three of whom were girls.

The establishment of relationships with Erasmus and, at the same time, with the other English Humanists produced something of a crisis in More's life. His alienation from the law became more pronounced, and he contemplated the taking of monastic vows that would leave him free to pursue the learning that had become his passion. For long periods, in the years between 1500 and 1504, he lived in a monastery, the Charterhouse of London, and devoted himself to the study of Greek and of the

---

[1] In the nineteenth century the Cathedral school was moved from the City out to suburban West Kensington; and was housed in a gloomy Gothic prison where the sun rarely penetrated, where a child might be flogged for a petty offense, and where the discipline of the grammarians drove away the light of learning. Colet's passionate motto—*aut doce aut disce aut discede*—remained emblazoned over the portals of the dull Victorian school.

early Church fathers, with Grocyn and Linacre as his teachers. John More's resolute opposition finally put an end to this, and he was in a position to enforce his will since he still controlled the purse strings. In the years following, Thomas returned to the workaday world; after 1504 we find him launched on a secular career—married, a member of the House of Commons, a prosperous lawyer, undersheriff of London—but finding time despite his numerous responsibilities for the continued pursuit of classical studies and for composition both in Latin and in English.

In 1509 Henry VII died and the young Henry VIII ascended the throne. The Humanists had already established relations with the young prince and their brightest dreams of peace and social reform centered around the person of the royal youth; but their hopes of having found a wise and enlightened ruler to execute their policies were speedily dashed. In 1511 the young king, now under the tutelage of Thomas Wolsey, joined the "Holy League" of Aragon, Venice and Pope Julius II; preparations for war were set on foot that culminated in the invasion of France in 1513, and Flodden Field. In that same year, 1511, More experienced private sorrow as well as deep concern over the course of public affairs. His first wife, Jane Holt, died, leaving him alone with four small children to care for. He remarried at once for the sake of his family rather than for love, taking as his wife Alice Middleton, a widow some years older than himself.

In 1515 More was sent, at the request of the London wool merchants, on a mission to the Continent, accompanying Cuthbert Tunstall, later Bishop of London, and Richard Sampson, a diplomat, as a delegation whose purpose it was to reopen the wool trade between England and the Netherlands. This trade had been interrupted that year as a result of an embargo on the export of wool that had been imposed by Henry VIII himself for political reasons. The negotiations, for reasons that need not be entered into here, were tedious, complex and difficult; More was obliged to prolong his absence from home for six months, which was far longer than he had originally expected. During the weeks of boredom and of waiting, he found distraction, as he tells us in the first book of *Utopia,* in the company of Peter Giles, the town clerk of Antwerp and the good friend of Erasmus; and he eased the pangs of homesickness and the painful yearning for his family by composing the second and major part of *Utopia.* He returned to England at the end of 1515, completed his manuscript in the first months of 1516, and entrusted it to Erasmus. The first edition was published at Louvain in 1517.

Utopia appeared less than three years after Niccolò Machiavelli had written *The Prince. The Prince* was written as a guide to the Medici overlords of Florence in their quest for autocratic power; it was a piece of political advice given directly to the autocrat, and no evasions or circumlocutions were necessary. But *Utopia* had a far different purpose. It was designed as an exposure of the evils afflicting men precisely because they were obliged to live under the rule of tyrants. It addressed itself, not to the exaltation of the power of princes, but to the elimination of crying abuses for which princes were at least in part responsible. *Utopia* was written in Latin and addressed in the first instance to a limited circle of scholars, clerics and statesmen. In literary form it was part dialogue, part traveler's tale. Its dangerous and outlandish ideas, including a biting attack on the evils of English life, were placed in the mouth of an imaginary character, Raphael Hythloday. More's genius endows the whole with such vitality that both the people in the dialogue and the imaginary country beyond the seas, Utopia, come very much alive. Fact and fiction must have been exceedingly hard for contemporary readers to have separated in an age when every homebound boat brought tales of new and incredible wonders in the New World beyond the Atlantic. Even in our own day there are those who insist that More's tale is a truthful and factual account of social conditions existing somewhere at that time.[2]

Utopia is divided into two parts. In the first of these More sets the stage by introducing his principal character, Raphael Hythloday. He tells us that he had met this mariner at the house of Peter Giles of Antwerp during the ambassadorial mission to Flanders from which he had just returned. Through the mouth of Hythloday, More launches into a brilliant critique of the social and political order in England. He raises the question: how is a wise man to seek remedies for the evils that he sees around him? With fine impartiality he deals out blows at degenerate and lazy priests, cruel, selfish and power-crazed kings, at the institution of private property, and the laws that sustain it. He holds up to scorn men so driven by the lust for gold and the trappings of wealth that they will allow nothing, neither the love of man nor the fear of God, to curb their drive to attain their selfish, antisocial goals.

---

[2] Arthur E. Morgan, *Nowhere Was Somewhere* (Community Service: Raleigh, N.C., 1947), argues on slim evidence that More was giving a factual account of sixteenth-century Peru.

In the second part of *Utopia* More sketches out a purely imaginary society where the altruistic ideals of a shared life and not the selfish ones of private acquisition are dominant. In Utopia there is no private property in the means of production—that is, the land, mines, harbor facilities, tools and other productive instruments which constitute the economic basis of social existence. Even the dwelling houses are communally owned and residence in them is rotated. Work in Utopia is compulsory for all able-bodied men and women. There is no sympathy for idlers; they are punished with forced labor. Where necessary, jobs are assigned to people in accordance with the needs of the state. There is no money: economic production is not undertaken for monetary or for any other kind of private profit. The produce of the people's labor is placed in warehouses, and distribution is planned in accordance with need. Each community maintains its own hospitals, and the sick are cared for and fed at the common charge. The preparation and cooking of food is an industry for which provision is made like any other. Population is carefully controlled by planned emigration and immigration, and is maintained at a predetermined level that has a definite relationship to Utopia's economic resources and its labor requirements. Cities are of uniform design; a high value is placed on city planning and a beautiful, healthy and dignified environment. The aged and the very young are treated with kindness and provided for like everyone else.

Some commentators have argued that the Utopian economy is an economy of scarcity, and that the frugality of Utopian life differentiates Utopia radically from social systems that set themselves the goal of material abundance for all.[3] Yet More tells us explicitly that *with equality of wealth all men have everything in abundance.* It is true that this abundance is achieved by a restriction of needs—Utopian society concerns itself with the full satisfaction of basic needs and not with the manufacture of new needs. The expansion of material needs and the allocation of time and labor to make possible their satisfaction is sacrificed deliberately for the sake of something else upon which the Utopians place the highest value: leisure. Leisure is distinguished from idleness; the Utopians have a passion for learning and self-improvement, and they believe that leisure must be used for the cultivation of the mind. In all of this we see a perfectly rational economic decision; that is, a decision to use labor to achieve abundance of leisure to be used for the pursuit of noneconomic ends.

Thus we must characterize Utopia as an economy of rude plenty. Even gold, which the Utopians despise, they have abundance of, and use it to make manacles and chamber pots, and to hire foreign mercenaries. The supreme good which this economy makes possible is the untrammeled pursuit of the philosophic life.

Utopia is permeated by a strong spirit of democratic republicanism. The first book is remarkable for its onslaught upon kings who pursue their own selfish interests rather than the welfare of their people. More enunciated the democratic doctrine that the true function of government is to serve the people and to promote their well-

---

[3] J. H. Hexter, for example, argues that the restriction of wants is "an integral element in the pattern of More's social thought," differentiating Utopia from the modern socialist economy, the aim of which is "the optimum satisfaction of wants." *More's Utopia* (Princeton University Press: Princeton, 1952), pp. 66–71.

being and happiness. The Utopian system and way of life, More tells us, has been shaped by the laws and influence of its founding father, Utopus; but the country is remarkable in the explicit absence of absolute rulers and of autocratic rule. It is run by a democratically elected assembly of 162 members; local government is in the hands of magistrates chosen directly or indirectly as the representatives of the families comprising the community. Equality prevails in Utopia; there is no class of idlers, drones who receive an income from the labor of others without performing any social service themselves. The Utopians are not infested with swarms of monks, priests and friars; the priests, More tells us, are elected by secret ballot, and there are only thirteen of them in each city, "very saintly and hence very few." Women receive the same education and the same rights as men. Punishment is meted out in proportion to the gravity of the crime. War is presented as the greatest of crimes, essentially a crime committed by rulers against their unoffending subjects, a social sin rising from human greed and pride.

In matters of religion the Utopians demonstrate a deep respect for individual rights. All forms of worship and all types of belief about God are permitted, something entirely befitting a people not yet vouchsafed Christian revelation. Violent or aggressive propaganda in favor of a particular religious dogma is viewed as a dangerous source of discord and is punishable by bondage or exile. All Utopians are required to believe in the immortality of the soul and the existence of God, but there is no punishment for nonbelief. The propaganda of atheism, even as the propaganda of religious dogma, is forbidden.

What is the meaning of *Utopia*?

Interpretations of More's social fantasy have been both numerous and conflicting, ranging from the views of Catholic theologians and philosophers on the one side to Marxist historians on the other. Marxist interpretation received its first and most able formulation in the work of Karl Kautsky, leader and theoretician of the German Social Democratic Party.[4] Kautsky saw *Utopia* as a vision of the socialist society of the future; he hailed its author as a farsighted spokesman of the modern working class at a time when that class had scarcely even begun to appear on the historical scene. More, in Kautsky's view, was a Catholic champion of social revolution who wished to eliminate the glaring evils of the late medieval world. It was, according to Kautsky, More's greatness to grasp the causal connection between the institution of private property and the poverty, violence and oppression to which humanity was subjected. And it was More's tragedy to stand alone, to sacrifice life itself for his convictions, at a time when there was no way to put into practice the conclusions to which his thought had brought him.

Criticism of Kautsky's position has been made by recent Marxist writers, notably Russell Ames, and this will be examined later in the discussion.[5] Traditional Catholic interpretation of More has controverted Kautsky not so much by a head-on attack upon his views as by the presentation of a radically different theory. Catholic spokesmen have long argued that More, far from being bent upon the destruction of the medieval world, was on the contrary its champion and defender. His views on

---

[4] Karl Kautsky, *Thomas More and His Utopia* (Russell & Russell, Inc.: New York, 1959), originally issued in English translation in 1890.
[5] See p. xviii.

communism and private property have been explained as an expression of the medieval monastic ideal, in which Christian men and women took vows of poverty and chastity, shared all things in common, and devoted themselves through prayer and good works to the service of the poor and the sick.[6] According to this view *Utopia* was purely a defense of the medieval order against the commercialism and self-seeking of an age that was tearing it apart.

The difficulty with this position is that it can be defended only by ignoring More's sweeping condemnation of *all* private property. Monastic orders were, at best, mere enclaves in a medieval society based upon the private ownership of land, upon a stratified social structure and upon the more or less crude exploitation of the serfs. More's theory is a theory of society, of an obligatory political association, not of a voluntary religious grouping. The *general* application to medieval life of the early Christian or monastic ideal would have meant quite simply the abolition of the medieval order. In *Utopia*, furthermore, it is made clear that the religious or monastic orders play a useful but subordinate role. Their practitioners scorn leisure and ease, and undertake the hardest and dirtiest work for the sake of providing more leisure for others.

Of recent years both Marxists and Catholics have considerably modified the traditional interpretations. Russell Ames has attacked Kautsky's presentation of More as a "representative of the proletariat." More was under-sheriff of London, and had many intimate connections with the prosperous merchants of that city. He was, con-

---

cludes Ames, a "middle class man" and his thinking represented the concerns of his own class. Ames argues, consequently, that in *Utopia* the socialist concern with the abolition of private property is incidental and subordinate. More, says this writer, was not a socialist, but a middle-class republican who sought to reform feudal society along republican and democratic lines.[7]

Ames's approach can be sustained only at the cost of ignoring things that cannot be ignored. *Utopia* attacks private property in its entirety. It is difficult to see how this position can be reconciled with the presentation of More as a representative of a class of people owning private property. The same point may be made more specifically by reference to the enclosure movement. The heart of More's attack in Book One of *Utopia* is directed against enclosures. There had set in, in the late fourteenth century, a movement in the English countryside which, over the course of the following three centuries, was to transform not only the structure and organization of farming but was to bring about revolutionary changes in the ownership of the land itself. The enclosure movement was an extremely complex affair, and may not readily be summarized in a few sentences; basically it involved the transformation of the feudal system of landownership, the elimination from the countryside of tens of thousands of tenant farmers, the conversion of arable land to pasture, and above all, the expropriation of common lands by a small minority of owners, and their consolidation into huge estates in the interest of raising commercial crops and extracting from them a monetary

---

[7] Russell Ames, *Citizen Thomas More and His Utopia* (Princeton University Press: Princeton, N.J., 1949).

profit. This movement, it is true, had not progressed very far when More wrote *Utopia*, but far enough that its salient outlines and its implications for the future were clear to him. More raised his voice in protest against property owners who through the use of force, threats, trickery and the power of the law stole land from those weaker than themselves, and subjected these to starvation and destitution for the purpose only of their own private, selfish gain.

More's attack on the enclosure movement remains the part of *Utopia* best remembered and most often quoted. It is inescapably an attack not only on the enclosure movement itself but upon that—in More's view—wicked and greedy class of men responsible for initiating it and carrying it through. Russell Ames recognizes that More is here making a direct onslaught upon sixteenth-century property owners.[8] But he is unable to provide a satisfactory explanation of how this is to be reconciled with a presentation of More as a representative of this same property-owning class.[9]

Of recent years there has appeared an interpretation of More that proclaims as its purpose his "rescue" from Catholic and Marxist alike. J. H. Hexter [10] presents More as a humanist and moralist who is concerned not so much with community of property and the economic reorgani-

---

[8] *Citizen Thomas More;* p. 116.

[9] More, argues Ames, "sought to lead the middle class along progressive paths." *Ibid.,* p. 104. The meaning of this statement is not made clear. The "progressive path" that More advocates with such force in *Utopia* leads to the elimination of property and property owners alike. This is hardly to be classed as friendly advice, nor can the one who gives it be considered a representative of property owners or of their interests.

[10] *More's Utopia: the Biography of an Idea* (Princeton University Press: Princeton, N.J., 1952), pp. 66–81.

zation of society as with the conquest of the sin of pride. More believes, he says, that pride is laid deep in man's nature, and it finds fatal outlets in the accumulation of material wealth, in ostentatious display. When it fully rules the human soul, pride seeks gratification if necessary at the cost of human life and welfare itself. More's socialism, according to Hexter, is an ascetic system designed to curb pride by taking away the instrumentalities —money and property—without which it is unable to find gratification. In *Utopia,* then, the economic function is subordinate and incidental; the common life and community of property fulfill a purely moral purpose. Humanist and moralist, More is not a defender of the medieval order; and he has little in common with modern Marxists. Whereas the Marxist believes that the abolition of private property will ultimately eradicate all antisocial behavior, More believes that pride is deeply ingrained in human nature and that the moral struggle against it will never end. "The Utopian Discourse," concludes Hexter, "is the production of a Christian humanist uniquely endowed with a statesman's eye and mind, a broad worldly experience, and a conscience of unusual sensitivity, who saw sin and especially the sin of pride as the cancer of the commonwealth." [11]

The problem with this particular interpretation of More is its instability; it is so easy for it to disintegrate into something else. This is well illustrated in the Catholic approach as recently revised by Father Edward Surtz.[12] Father Surtz cheerfully concedes that Utopia is

[11] *Ibid.,* p. 78.
[12] Father Edward Surtz, S.J., *The Praise of Pleasure,* and *The Praise of Wisdom* (Harvard University Press: Cambridge, Mass., and Loyola University Press: Chicago, respectively; 1957).

a communist state. But what he gives with one hand he at once proceeds to take away with the other. More's *theoretical* acceptance of Jesus' teaching on the community of goods and the shared life, he says, is complemented by a conviction that, *in actual practice,* such teaching flies in the face of the facts of human nature and primarily the cold reality of man's fallen estate. "In his heart," concludes Father Surtz, "More realizes that his Utopian Commonwealth, like the republic of Plato, will never exist in the Christian West, unless the perfect sons of the perfect God are born to dwell therein. The ideal Christian Utopia must wait until men become ideal Christians. . . ." [13] The plain inference is that this will never happen, not, at least, until some of us get to Heaven. *Utopia,* then, is a moral tract, not a revolutionary manual. It teaches us to strive for poverty of spirit and brotherly love. [14]

Thus Hexter's position—that *Utopia* is a moral tract teaching us the necessity for a struggle against pride— leads him straight into the waiting arms of those very Catholics from whom he was striving to escape. As for More, he remains in the hands of the Catholics: the "rescue" is a failure.

We might forgive Hexter if, though failing to rescue More from the Catholics, he had succeeded in rescuing his hero from the Marxists. But in this he succeeds no better. We may believe, with the Catholics, that pride is an attribute of fallen man, and will be with him always

---

[13] *The Praise of Pleasure,* p. 190.
[14] *Ibid.,* p. 191. Father Surtz's works, charmingly and clearly written, have done much to illumine More as social reformer, as man of the Renaissance and as Catholic Humanist.

while he is on earth; or we may believe that pride, like other human faults, has a social origin and cause, rather than a transcendental one. What More believed about this himself, as a Catholic, is at the moment immaterial. It was his contribution to point out the *causal* connection between the problem of evil in the world and the economic factor in life. It is precisely from this that More's insistence upon the necessity for community of property derives its significance. More is saying that private property in any form establishes the roots and the foundation of pride, acquisitiveness and the destruction of human brotherhood. Abolish private property, he says, and you eliminate the fundamental condition that generates pride and its various forms in violence, hatred, injustice, oppression and war. More understands, further, that steps are necessary, not only to establish a given social order, but to defend, maintain and perpetuate it. Utopia is hedged around with a system of political and moral sanctions designed expressly to prevent the *reintroduction* of private property; conspiracy to change the constitution or the political regime is punishable by death, and those who shirk the duty of work are reduced to forced labor. The Utopians, too, are skilled in the arts of war, which they use zealously to ward off aggression.

In all of this, unfortunately for Hexter, More is in agreement with the Marxists, who conceive of the state as an instrumentality for the defense and perpetuation of the socialist system; and for the inculcation of the new system of moral values which it represents.

What, then, or whom, does More represent? The early Christian ideal as embodied in medieval society? The small band of Humanist scholars bent upon the reform of Christendom in the sixteenth century? The London merchants and enclosing landowners? The socialist movement that was to come?

Thomas More, undoubtedly, was deeply *influenced* by a variety of factors in his own heritage and in the society of his own times. Some of these factors have already been noted: Catholic and Christian concepts of equality and brotherhood, the Humanist critique of contemporary society, the democratic and antimonarchical attitudes of the Third Estate, the harsh oppression of the masses everywhere apparent in Tudor England. But to be *influenced* by such factors is not the same thing as "*representing*" any one of them in a narrow and exclusive sense. An original thinker is more than the sum of the ideas and the forces that influence him. He presents his concepts and his conclusions to humanity as an independent contribution, existing in its own right. More was such an original thinker. It is his greatness to have transcended the local biases and class prejudices of his own day and to have made an offering to human thought so permanent and so profound that the history of political philosophy in the Western world cannot fully be grasped without a comprehension of what he thought and said.

More's conclusions from *Utopia* are explicit enough. Men who wish to lead the good life—and *a fortiori* Christians who wish to seek salvation—must strive for the abolition of private self-seeking and the creation of a society where all things are shared. Otherwise greed, acquisitiveness, violence, robbery, poverty and crime —the catalogue of crimes that More summarizes in the one word "pride"—will interpose an impenetrable curtain between the soul and its destiny in this world and the next.[15]

For Thomas More, then, the objectives presented by social science were clear enough. But how were these objectives to be realized? What social leverage was available to enable reformers to carry their vision into practice? Here Humanists like More faced severe difficulties. Looking about them, they saw a society dominated by the fever of private acquisition, a society in which men, apart from the tiny band of dreamers of which More was one, were divided into rulers and ruled, oppressors and oppressed, rich and poor. Of these two classes the first were too selfish, the latter too ignorant and downtrodden, to heed the good advice which the Humanists had to tender to them.

The dilemma of political and social tactics finds expression in the first book of *Utopia*, pages 26-36, which was written after More's return to England from the Netherlands, and to which passage Hexter has given the name "dialogue of counsel." In this dialogue, More debates the issue of whether or no to take service with the King. To the question of whether royal power was or could be the instrumentality for the introduction of a reformed society, More answers with an emphatic "no." Kings, he says, and the fawning flatterers who surround them will not take good advice seriously; the only advice that they want and will use is how best to do the evil things that they have already set their hearts upon. ". . . there is no place," concludes Hythloday, "for philos-

---

[15] ". . . the whole world," cries Hythloday, "could easily have been brought long ago to the laws of Utopia by the consideration of each man's advantage or by the authority of our Saviour Christ . . . if that single beast —the chief and parent of all plagues—pride did not fight against it." See p. xxv.

ophy with kings. . . . For with a king there is no place for dissimulation or conniving. One must openly praise the vilest plans and put one's signature to the most disastrous decrees. He would be considered a spy and almost a traitor who gave faint praise to wicked decisions."

With these words More wrote his own epitaph. Under strong pressure, against his own better judgment and the clear conclusion of his own thought in *Utopia*, he permitted himself to be drawn into the service of Henry VIII and the court in 1518.[16] For a while matters went reasonably well. In 1517 Martin Luther had nailed his theses to the church door at Wittenberg; More turned his pen to the service of the Catholic faith and its defense from the heresy that would divide and destroy Christendom. On this issue Henry VIII and More found themselves at first upon the same side; More's polemical efforts, ironically enough, earned for Henry the title "Defender of the Faith." But in 1527 Henry changed sides. Driven by his passion for Anne Boleyn, the need for a male heir whom his wife Catherine evidently could not supply, and the necessity for a divorce which the Pope was powerless to grant, Henry repudiated papal authority, declared himself head of the Church in England, and thus procured the nullification of his marriage that he had hitherto vainly sought.

In 1529 More had been appointed Lord Chancellor in the place of Thomas Wolsey, and in this capacity he was called upon to give his approval to the divorce action. But he refused to recognize what he considered a grossly arbitrary step taken by his sovereign. In More's view, the Pope, and no other, was the head of the Church; no

---

[16] For the possible reasons for More's contradictory behavior, see Kautsky, pp. 139–42, and Hexter, pp. 132–55.

temporal monarch could rightfully arrogate to himself a title which could only serve to increase an already extensive political power and make him guardian of the religion and conscience as well as the political destinies of his people. More, accordingly, resigned the Chancellorship in 1532 and refused steadfastly to give his sanction to the Act of Supremacy passed in 1534. Executed for high treason on July 6, 1535, he stands as one of the great figures of the ages who sacrificed life itself rather than yield integrity of conscience and inner conviction to the behest of a tyrant.

In canonizing Thomas More, the Church gave the seal of its approval to the whole man, not a part of him. Not a little of the spirit of More is to be found in the encyclical *Pacem in Terris* issued by John XXIII in 1963. Both teach that all men, even pagans, are children of God, and that their seemingly outlandish social experiments must be regarded by true Christians with reverence and respect.

BIBLIOGRAPHY

Published Works and Correspondence

THOMAS MORE wrote voluminously, both in Latin and in English. Much of this material has for centuries been unavailable to the ordinary student. More often than not the Latin writings have been unavailable in translation, and difficult to come by in the original; the English works have existed only in the rare edition published by More's son-in-law, William Rastell, in 1557. A useful listing of More's writings as published in the two centuries following his death is available in R. W. Gibson, *Sir Thomas More: Preliminary Bibliography to 1750* (Yale University Press: New Haven, Conn., 1961). *Utopia,* of course, has always been the exception in this situation. Over the years it has been translated into many languages and has been published in numerous editions both in England and in the United States.

The last forty years have witnessed an effort to bring back More's literary heritage to the English-speaking public. W. E. Campbell inaugurated a project to reissue the 1557 edition of *The English Works,* and two volumes of seven planned were published in 1927 and 1931 with modern English versions and copious editorial commentary. Here the reader will find the famous *History of Richard III* (Vol. I), and the *Dialogue Concerning Tyndale* (Vol. II); but World War II put an end to this project, and it has not been resumed. The other most notable contribution of this recent period is Elizabeth Frances Rogers' *The Correspondence of Sir Thomas More* (Princeton University Press: Princeton, N.J., 1947). This is a work for the specialist; the Latin letters—a majority of all More's correspondence—remain untranslated, or translations made in previous years and now largely inaccessible are not provided. The English letters are given with the archaic spelling and terminology of Tudor English. The general reader will find the same editor's *St. Thomas More: Selected Letters* (Yale University Press: New Haven, Conn., 1961) satisfying as a modernized introduction to More's correspondence.

Other portions of More's writings reissued of recent years include *Sir Thomas More's History of the Passion*, translated by his granddaughter Mary Basset, edited by Mgr. P. E. Hallett (London, 1941); *The Supplication of Souls*, edited by Mary Thecla (Westminster, Md., 1950); *Prayers While He Was a Prisoner in the Tower of London*, edited by E. F. Rogers (Madison, N.J., 1952); *The Apology*, edited by Arthur Irving Taft (Oxford, 1930); and the *Latin Epigrams*, edited with translation by L. Bradner and C. A. Lynch (Chicago, 1953).

Yale University Press has announced a complete scholarly edition of More's writings in fourteen volumes, with English translations and notes, and an edition of selected works in modern English in seven volumes. Such a plan carried effectively to completion will supersede all previous editions of More's writings. The individual volumes are being issued 1961–1971.

Biographies

Thomas More has been much written about, and it is

scarcely surprising that a complete listing of such works is not available, though a great deal of ground is covered in the helpful *Moreana 1478–1945: a Preliminary Check List of Material by and about Sir Thomas More,* compiled by Frank and M. P. Sullivan (Kansas City, Mo., 1946).

Of the earliest biographies, various editions of William Roper's *The Life of Sir Thomas More* have appeared. The most recent and the most useful appears in a work edited by Richard S. Sylvester and Davis F. Harding entitled *Two Early Tudor Lives* (Yale University Press: New Haven and London, 1962). Roper's *Life* is one of the books about More that the modern student should read first. It retains a permanent value as a picture of the man seen through the eyes of one who was a member of his intimate household for sixteen years. A modern work that achieves the same result through the use of dramatic form is Robert Bolt's powerful play *A Man for All Seasons* (Random House, Inc., New York, 1962).

Numerous other biographical studies of More have appeared. The most valuable of the longer treatments are T. E. Bridgett, *The Life of Blessed Thomas More* (London, 1891), and R. W. Chambers, *Thomas More* (New York, 1936). Among the shorter sketches Leslie Paul, *Sir Thomas More* (Roy Publishers, Inc.: London and New York, n.d.) provides a useful summary of the main events of More's life and literary career. In general no biography of More may be considered adequate that fails to set its subject fairly and squarely in the life of his own times and in the perspective of Renaissance Europe and the Humanist tradition. The following works make an important contribution in this respect: Frederic Seebohm, *The Oxford Reformers,* a pioneer study that appeared in 1869 and was reissued in the Everyman edition, London and

New York, 1914, and subsequent printings; E. M. G. Routh, *Sir Thomas More and his Friends, 1477–1535* (Russell & Russell, Inc.), originally published 1934 and reissued New York, 1963; W. E. Campbell, *Erasmus, Tyndale, and More* (Dufour editions, London and Milwaukee, 1949); Fritz Caspari, *Humanism and the Social Order in Tudor England* (Chicago, 1954); Pearl Hogrefe, *The Sir Thomas More Circle* (University of Illinois Press: Urbana, Ill., 1959); and Robert P. Adams, *The Better Part of Valor: More, Erasmus, Colet, and Vives on Humanism, War, and Peace, 1496–1535* (University of Washington Press: Seattle, Wash., 1962). More's status as a polemical writer receives detailed commentary in Rainer Pineas, *Thomas More's English Writings of Religious Commentary*, unpublished doctoral dissertation, Columbia University, 1958.

Utopia

Karl Kautsky fired the opening gun in the modern controversy over the meaning of *Utopia* in *Thomas More and His Utopia*, first published in English in 1890 and reissued New York, 1959, by Russell & Russell, Inc. Russell Ames, *Citizen Thomas More and His Utopia* (Princeton University Press: Princeton, N.J., 1949), attempted an extension and correction of Kautsky's views. Traditional Catholic interpretations are Bridgett and Chambers, cited above, and W. E. Campbell, *More's Utopia and His Social Teaching* (London, 1930). J. H. Hexter, *More's Utopia: the Biography of an Idea* (Princeton University Press: Princeton, N.J., 1952), tried to steer a middle course between medievalist and Marxist interpretations, but with indifferent success. Hexter's work is a tour de force remarkable not so much for a fresh interpretation of *Utopia* as for its analysis of the structure of the document and of the significance in it of what Hexter terms the "dialogue of counsel."

Hexter's Humanist interpretation of More is close to that of the Catholic revisionist Father Edward Surtz. The latter's position has been developed in two books of careful and stimulating commentary: *The Praise of Pleasure* (Harvard University Press: Cambridge, Mass., 1957) and *The Praise of Wisdom* (Loyola University Press: Chicago, 1957).

Tudor England

The following helpful references to the political and social background of the early Tudor period may be mentioned. R. H. Tawney, *The Agrarian Problem in the Sixteenth Century* (Franklin Book Programs, Inc.: London, 1912), is a classic of early enclosure history. J. A. Williamson, *The Tudor Age* (David McKay Co., Inc.: London and New York, 1953); H. A. L. Fisher, *History of England 1485–1547* (London, 1934); and J. D. Mackie, *The Earlier Tudors, 1485–1558* (Oxford University Press: Oxford, 1953), all provide useful facts on the reigns of Henry VII and VIII. Garrett Mattingley, *Catherine of Aragon* (Boston, 1941) furnishes a colorful account of the royal divorce crisis.

BOOK ONE

THE MOST VICTORIOUS King of England, Henry the Eighth, most accomplished in all the virtues of an outstanding prince, recently had a disagreement on certain matters of great importance with Charles, the most serene Prince of Castile. To settle and arrange this dispute, the King sent me as ambassador to Flanders, together with that incomparable man Cuthbert Tunstall, whom, to everyone's great joy, he recently made Master of the Rolls. But of this man's virtues I shall say nothing, not because I am afraid that a friend's evidence should be considered suspect, but because his goodness and learning are too great to be praised by me, and also too well known and famous everywhere to need my praise; unless, as the saying goes, I should wish to seem to be illuminating the sun with a lantern.

As had been arranged, all those excellent gentlemen met us at Bruges who had been entrusted with the affair by their prince. The chief and head of these was the Margrave of Bruges, a most distinguished gentleman. But their learned spokesman was George de Theimsecke, Provost of Kassel, a man eloquent by training and nature, greatly skilled in law and an unrivaled master in debating affairs both by his natural genius and by his constant experience in practical matters. We met once or twice, but could not sufficiently agree on certain points; so they said good-bye to us for a few days and left for Brussels to find out what their prince had in mind. Meanwhile I set off to Antwerp; for so my affairs demanded.

While I was staying there, I had visits from several people, but none was more welcome than Peter Giles, a native of Antwerp. He is a man of great honesty and high position among his people, worthy of the highest. I cannot say which is greater, his learning or his excellence of character; for he is of the highest quality and deeply read in literature, with an open heart to everyone. Toward his friends he is so affectionate, loving, faithful and sincere that you could scarcely find one or two people anywhere whom you would feel comparable to him in all respects of friendship. He has a rare modesty and no one could be less pretentious, no one could possess a wiser simplicity. Further, he is so graceful in talk and so harmlessly witty that by his sweet company and delightful conversation he greatly alleviated my longing for my own country and home, my wife and my children, whom I was restless to see again as I had already been away from home for more than four months.

One day I had attended Mass in the Cathedral of Notre Dame, a most beautiful building, always crowded with people. When the service was finished, I was preparing to return to the place where I was staying, when I happened to see Peter Giles conversing with a stranger, a man approaching old age, with a sunburned face and a long beard, whose cloak was carelessly hanging from his shoulder. From his appearance and dress I judged him to be a sailor. When Peter saw me, he came up and greeted me. As I was about to reply, he drew me aside a little distance, and said, "Do you see this man?" at the same time pointing out the man with whom I had seen him talking. "I intended," he said, "to bring him straight to you." "He would have been most welcome," I said, "for your sake." "No," said Peter, "for his own sake, if you knew him. For there is no one alive today who could tell you so much about unknown peoples and lands; and I know that you are most eager to hear about such things." "So," said I, "my guess was not far amiss. For at first glance I felt that the man was a sailor." "And yet," said Peter, "you are very wrong. For he sailed certainly, not like Palinurus, but like Ulysses, or rather, like Plato. Raphael Hythloday over there (for this is his name) has a great knowledge of Latin and a profound one of Greek. He paid more attention to Greek than Latin because he had devoted himself entirely to philosophy, and on this subject he knew that nothing of any importance is extant in Latin except a few things of Seneca and Cicero. Well, he left to his brothers the inheritance he had at home (he is Portuguese), and from a desire to see the world joined himself to Amerigo Vespucci. In the last three of those four voyages that everyone is reading about, he was Amerigo's constant companion, except that on the last voyage he did not return with him. For he, with the greatest difficulty, obtained permission from him to be among those twenty-three who at the end of the last voyage were left in the fort. And so he was left behind, as a concession to his mind, which cared more for foreign travel than a grave; for he was constantly repeating the sayings: 'Who does not have an urn is covered by the sky,' and 'The road to heaven is the same length from all directions.' His attitude would have cost him dearly, if God had not been favorable to him.

"After Vespucci left, he visited many regions with five companions from the fort, and by good fortune at last came to Ceylon and from there to Calicut. There he was lucky to find some Portuguese ships and at last, contrary to his expectations, he returned to his own country."

When Peter told me this, I thanked him for his kindness toward me for being so anxious that I should enjoy the talk of a man whose conversation he thought would be pleasant to me. Then I turned to Raphael. After an exchange of greetings and those pleasantries which people say on first meeting a stranger, we left that place and went to my house; and there in the garden we sat on a bench covered with green turf and began to talk together.

So he told us how he and his companions who had remained in the fort, after the departure of Vespucci, by kind approaches gradually won the favor of the natives of that land, and soon were able to move among them with no danger and with great ease, and how also they were regarded with great affection by a certain leader, whose country and name I have forgotten. By his generosity, he said, he and his five companions were given an abundance of supplies and money. For their journey (which was by boat on the water and by chariot on land) they were also given a very trusty guide to take them to other leaders whom they wished to see, and were supplied with the highest commendations. After traveling for many days, he said, he discovered towns and cities, and populous republics with excellent constitutions.

For under the Equator, and on both sides of it, for the distance taken in by the movement of the sun, there lie great deserts parched with constant heat. Everywhere the land is rough and harsh to the sight, terrible, untended, inhabited by wild beasts and serpents, or else men no less wild than the beasts nor less dangerous. But when you have traveled farther, gradually everything grows more gentle: the climate is less harsh, the land pleasantly green, the animals more mild. Eventually you meet peoples, cities, towns. In these there is constant commerce by land and sea, not merely among themselves and their neighbors, but also with far distant countries.

From there he had the opportunity to visit many lands far and wide, because he and his companions were readily welcomed on any ship that was being fitted out for any journey. He said that the ships they saw in the first regions had a flat keel; their sails were made from stitched reeds or osiers, in some places leather. But afterward they came across pointed keels and canvas sails, in short, everything like ours. Their sailors have a great knowledge of the sea and the sky.

But he said he won great favor by showing them how to use the magnet. They had been previously quite ignorant of this, and consequently had been afraid to venture on the sea and did so only in the summer. But now, relying on the magnet, they are not worried by the winter, quite without fear but not without danger; for there is a great hazard that the very thing which they thought would bring them great good may, through their lack of prudence, be the cause of great ills.

He related what he saw in each place, but it would be too long for me to tell it all, and is not the purpose of this work. Perhaps I shall repeat it in another place, especially what it would be profitable to know; above all, those just and wise provisions which he observed among peoples continually living together in harmony. For we asked eagerly about these matters and he gladly discoursed on them. But we did not inquire about monsters, for there is nothing unusual about this subject. For everywhere you can find Scyllas and greedy Celaenos and man-eating Laestrygonians, and fearsome monsters of that kind; but people governed by healthy and wise laws cannot be found just anywhere.

But just as he observed many foolish practices among those new peoples, so he also told us of many institutions from which we might take suitable examples for correcting the errors of these cities, nations, peoples and kingdoms of ours. As I said, I shall relate these in another place. For the moment I want to repeat only what he said about the ways and institutions of the Utopians. But first I will give the conversation which gradually led us to the mention of that republic.

Raphael had first with great wisdom touched upon the various mistakes both in our world and in that new one (and certainly they are very numerous in both places). Then he mentioned the wiser provisions that both we and they have. He so thoroughly understood the ways and practices of each people that it seemed that he had spent his whole life in whatever place he visited. In amazement at the man, Peter said, "My dear Raphael, I am surprised that you do not join yourself to some king. I am quite sure that you would be in great favor with any king, since by this learning and knowledge of places and men you could not merely give pleasure but also instruct by examples and aid by your advice. In this way you would look after your own interests admirably and also be able to help your family and friends greatly."

"As to my family and friends," he said, "I am not much

worried, since I think that I have fulfilled my obligations toward them well enough. For other people do not part with their possessions unless they are old and sick, and even then with reluctance when they can no longer hold on to them; but I shared mine out to my family and friends not only when I was healthy and lively, but also when I was a young man. I think they ought to be content with this liberality of mine, and not demand and expect in addition that for their sakes I should give myself into servitude to kings."

"God forbid," said Peter. "My intention was that you should go not into servitude but into service of kings." "That" said he, "is only one syllable less than servitude." "But whatever name you give to it," said Peter, "my opinion is that this is the very road by which you could not only bring profit to others, both privately and publicly, but also make your own condition more prosperous."

"Should I make myself more prosperous," said Raphael, "by the road I find repulsive? And yet now I live just as I wish—a blessing which I suspect comes to very few men in high positions. But there are enough men of that kind who court the friendship of the powerful. So do not think it any great loss if they are going to do without me and one or two like me."

Then I said, "It is clear, Raphael, that you desire neither wealth nor power; and I for one respect and look up to a man of your mind no less than any of those who are in powerful positions. But you will be acting in a way worthy of your noble and philosophic spirit if you so dispose yourself, even though it may involve some private disadvantage, as to lend your ability and industry to public affairs. This you could most profitably do if you

Princes + generally evil
Gov't.

were a counselor to some great prince, and (as I am sure
you would do) gave him advice both upright and honorable. For from a prince a river of all good or evil things
flows upon the whole people as if from some perpetual
fountain. But you have such perfect learning that even
without much experience you could make yourself an in-
dispensable counselor to any king, and such experience
of affairs that you could do so without any learning."

"My dear More," said he, "you are twice wrong, first
about me and secondly about the matter itself. For I do
not have the ability you attribute to me, and even if I
did, though I might disturb my own peace, I should not
advance the state at all. For in the first place, practically
all princes themselves take greater delight in spending
their time on military pursuits than on the good arts of
peace; and I neither have nor want skill in those matters.
They are much more concerned how to get new kingdoms for themselves, by fair means or foul, than to ad-
minister well what they already have. Moreover, all the
counselors of kings either are so wise as not to be in need
of another's advice, or else think themselves so wise that
they do not gladly welcome it. The only exception is
when they flatter and agree to all the most ridiculous re-
marks of men whom, because of their great influence
with the prince, they wish to win over by fawning. And
certainly it is a natural failing for a man to be pleased
with his own inventions. So a raven dotes on its chick
and a monkey loves its young.

"But suppose that in that company of people who
either are jealous of others' thoughts or prefer their own,
a man should bring something forward which he has
read of as done on other occasions, or has seen done in
other parts. Those who hear it act exactly as if their

whole reputation for wisdom were in danger, and as if after that they ought to be considered absolute fools if they cannot find some way to discredit others' discoveries. If all other means fail them, then they take refuge in saying, "These things pleased our forefathers. If only we could match their wisdom!" So with these words they are quite content, as if they had brought the discussion to a brilliant conclusion. As if it would involve terrible dangers if anyone were found wiser than his forefathers in any matter at all! Yet all their wisest decisions we are quite happy to let go; but if anywhere they might have made more prudent decisions, we eagerly fasten onto them, and hold on with our teeth. So I have come across these proud, stupid and bad-tempered judgments in many parts of the world, and in England too, once."

"Please tell me," said I. "Did you visit us?" "Yes," he said, "and I stayed there several months, not long after the western English rose in civil war against their king and were crushed with pitiful slaughter. During that time I was much indebted to the Right Reverend Father John Morton, Archbishop of Canterbury and Cardinal, and at that time Chancellor of England too. What I am about to say is well known to More, but believe me, Peter, he was a man worthy of the highest respect not more for his authority than for his wisdom and goodness. He was of moderate height and belied his advanced years. His face inspired reverence, not fear. In dealing with people he was easy, yet serious and dignified. It was his pleasure on occasions to speak harshly to those with requests to make of him, without any malice, just to find out what readiness of mind and spirit each man had. As long as a man kept away from impudence, he was delighted by such readiness, as being congenial to his own

nature, and he welcomed it as a quality appropriate to
a man of action. His conversation was polished and to
the point. He had great skill in law, an incomparable intellect and a prodigious memory. He had these virtues in
great abundance from birth, but he advanced them still
further by studying and practice.

"The King appeared to put great trust in his advice,
and the state to rely upon it heavily when I was there.
For practically from his early youth he was taken
straight from school to court and was employed in important matters all his life. Constantly tossed by the vary-
ing tides of fortune, he had with many great dangers
learned worldly wisdom. When it is won this way, it does
not easily leave.

"It happened one day that I was at his table, and a
certain layman was there, learned in your laws. On some
pretext or other he began loudly to sing the praises of
that stern justice which was then being used in England
against thieves, who, he said, were strung up everywhere,
sometimes twenty on one gallows. And so he said he was
all the more puzzled, when so few escaped punishment,
what evil fate produced so many robbers all over the
country. Then, presuming to speak freely in front of the
Cardinal, I said, 'There is no reason why you should be
surprised. For this punishment inflicted upon thieves is
beyond the bounds of justice and not to the public advantage. It is too severe for punishing robbery, but not
sufficient to restrain it. For simple theft is not so great a
crime as to deserve capital punishment, nor is there any
penalty strong enough to keep from theft men who have
no other means of gaining a livelihood. So in this matter
not only you, but a good part of this world also, seem
to copy bad teachers, who more readily beat their stu-

dents than educate them. For harsh and terrible punishments are inflicted upon thieves, when it would be much better to see that they had a means to earn a living. In this way they would be freed from the awful necessity of stealing and then being put to death.'

"'This has all been seen to well enough,' he said. 'There are manual crafts and there is farming: from these a man may support his life, unless by nature he prefers to be evil.' 'But you will not get out of it as easily as this,' I said. 'In the first place, let us forget those who often come home mutilated from foreign or civil wars, as recently happened among your people in the Cornish war, and not so long ago in France. These men give their limbs to their country or their king; their disability does not allow them to practice their former crafts, nor at such an age can they learn a new one. As I say, let us forget these, as wars come and go. Let us consider those cases that arise every day.

"'Now, there is a large number of noblemen who live in idleness like drones by the labors of others—in other words, they skin the tenants on their farms by increasing the rents. For that is the only thrift they know, though in other spheres they are so lavish as to beggar themselves. But as well as this, they take around an immense crowd of idle attendants, who have never learned any means of making a living. As soon as their master dies, or they themselves fall sick, they are thrown out straightaway. For masters are readier to support idlers than invalids, and often an heir cannot immediately afford the number of servants his dead father kept. Meanwhile they have the choice of violent hunger or violent robbery. For what are they to do? In wandering about, they wear out their clothes and health, and when they are unkempt with sickness and their clothes covered with patches, no gentleman deigns to receive them and no countryman dares. For they are well aware of the value of a man brought up softly in idleness and luxuries, who is used to sneering at the whole neighborhood with a braggart's look and despising everyone but himself, dressed up with his sword and shield. They know that he will be quite unsuited to be the faithful servant of a poor man, with a spade and a hoe, niggardly wages and scant food.'

" 'No,' he said, 'this is the kind of man we ought especially to cultivate. For these are men of higher and nobler spirit than craftsmen or farmers, and in them lies the power and strength of the army whenever a battle must be fought.'

" 'Of course,' I said, 'you might just as well say that we should cultivate thieves because of wars; for undoubtedly you will never be without wars as long as you have thieves. For neither are robbers fainthearted soldiers, nor are soldiers cowardly robbers; so nice an agreement is there between these two arts. But this is frequent among you, but not confined to you. For it belongs to practically all nations. Another more pestilential plague infests France as well; the whole country is filled and besieged with mercenary soldiers in peacetime too (if that can be called peace). They were brought in under the same belief through which you English thought that idle servants ought to be supported here: because, that is, the wise fools decided that the public safety depended upon the constant presence of a strong and firm garrison, especially of veterans. For they have no confidence in inexperienced men. The result is that they even have to seek out a war so as not to have unskilled soldiers, and wantonly to kill men so that (as Sallust wittily puts it) their hands or spirits may not grow dull through lack of practice.

"But how dangerous it is to keep beasts of this kind France has learned to her cost, and the same lesson is shown by the Romans, the Carthaginians, the Syrians and many other people. For their standing armies on various pretexts have overthrown their empires, and ravaged their country and cities. But how unnecessary this is can be seen from the example of the French: their soldiers, though trained to the fingertips, yet, when matched with your levies, cannot often boast that they have come off superior—I say no more, so as not to seem to flatter you to your face. But neither those city craftsmen of yours nor the rough and uncouth farmers are believed to be very afraid of the idle attendants of the noblemen—except for those who do not happen to have a body to match their strength and boldness, or whose strength of spirit is broken by poverty. So there is no danger that these attendants might grow soft if they were trained in honest crafts for their livelihood and exercised in manly work; for as it is now, their strong and robust bodies (nobles choose to corrupt only picked men) grow feeble with idleness or soft with womanly tasks. Certainly, whatever is the truth of this matter, of one thing I am quite sure: that it is by no means to the interest of the state to keep, against the possibility of a war which you never have except when you wish, an immense crowd of the sort that destroys the peace—and we ought to have much more consideration for peace than war.

"'But this is not the only reason which drives men to steal. There is another one more peculiar to you English in my opinion.' 'What is that?' said the Cardinal. 'Your sheep,' I said, 'which are normally so gentle and need so little food. Now (so they say) they have begun to be so ravenous and wild that they even eat up men. They devastate and destroy fields, houses and towns. For in whatever parts of the kingdom fine and therefore more precious wool is produced, there the nobles and gentlemen, and also some holy abbots, are not content with the rents and annual profits that their predecessors used to get from their farms. They are not satisfied to live in luxury and idleness and be of no use to the state; they even harm it. They leave nothing for arable land, enclose everything for pasture, destroy houses, tear down towns and leave only the church to house the sheep; and as if the forests and parks lost you too little ground, those good men turn all houses and cultivated land into a desert.

" 'Thus, so that one glutton, the insatiable and terrible plague of the country, may join together fields and enclose several thousand acres, some tenants are ejected. Others are stripped of their own land by trickery or violence, or, wearied by their wrongs, are driven to sell. And so, however it happens, the wretched people leave, men, women, husbands, wives, orphans, widows, parents with small children, and with their large, but impoverished, band of servants (as farming needs many hands); they leave, I say, the home they knew so well, nor can they find anywhere to go. All their furniture, which would not bring a high price even if it could wait for a buyer, they sell for a pittance, since it must go out. This money they soon spend on their wanderings. What is there left for them then except to steal and hang (justly, of course), or else roam and beg? Although even then they are thrown into prison as vagrants, because they are traveling around with nothing to do. For no one will hire their services, even though they offer them eagerly. For those accustomed to farming have nothing to do where no crops are sown. One shepherd or attendant is enough to graze the land with cattle, although formerly many hands were needed to cultivate it so as to ensure a good harvest.

"'And this is the reason why in many places food is much dearer. The price of wool too has risen so high that it just cannot be bought by the poor, who usually make their cloth from it in England; and for that reason more people are driven from work to idleness. For after the institution of the enclosures, the rot destroyed a very large number of sheep. It was as if God punished the owners' greed by sending destruction to the sheep, although it would have been juster if it had fallen on their own heads. But even if the number of sheep increases enormously, yet the price does not come down. For although there cannot be said to be a monopoly on sheep, since more than one man is engaged in selling them, they are certainly in the control of a very small number. For they have almost all fallen into the hands of a few rich men who are under no necessity to sell before they want, and who do not want to until they may at their own price. Now there is the same reason why the other kinds of cattle are equally dear, or even more so, since there is no one left to look after their reproduction now that the houses have been pulled down and farming is neglected. Nor do those rich men rear the young of the larger cattle as they do of the sheep. Instead they buy them cheaply when they are lean, fatten them up on their pastures and sell them again at a great price. So in my opinion the entire evil effect of this affair has not yet been felt. For until now they have been raising the prices only in these places where they sell; but when eventually they remove them more quickly than they can be born, then the supply will gradually decrease in the places where they are bought too, and a great and troublesome shortage will follow there.

" 'So now the wicked greed of a few has turned to a plague the very thing which made this island of yours seem so especially prosperous. For this dearness of food is the reason why everyone is dismissing as many servants as he can. Where are they going, I ask you, except to beg? Or on a course to which well-bred minds are more easily persuaded—to steal?

" 'Now beside this wretched poverty and need we find wanton luxury. For among the servants of noblemen, and the craftsmen and even the countrymen too, among people of all ranks, are found many new styles in clothing and an excessive lavishness in food. Now places of ill repute, brothels, whorehouses and stews, winehouses, alehouses, so many wicked games, dice, cards, the tables, tennis, bowls, quoits—these all quickly exhaust their money and send their devotees straight off somewhere to steal.

" 'Cast out these pernicious pests. Make a law that those who pulled them down should reconstruct the houses and country towns, or else give them up to people who are prepared to replace and rebuild them. Check the rich from buying everything up and put an end to their freedom in monopoly. Let fewer men be kept in idleness; bring back farming; reintroduce clothmaking to be an honorable business and a useful occupation for that idle mob, or for those whom until now poverty has

made thieves, or those who are now vagrants or idle
servants, both good material for future thieves. Certainly
if you do not heal these ills, your boasts of justice exercised in the punishment of theft are quite useless. This
justice in fact, is ostentatious rather than just or advantageous. When you allow people to be brought up in
the worst possible way and their characters to be gradually corrupted from a tender age, and then punish them
when they commit those crimes as men which they
showed all signs of doing from their childhood on—I ask
you, what else are you doing than making men thieves
and then punishing them?'

"While I was still saying this, the lawyer meanwhile
had seriously got himself ready to speak and had decided
to use that usual method of debaters who repeat men's
words with more care than they reply to them. In fact,
they have a very high regard for memory. 'Yes,' he said,
'a good speech for a foreigner. You have been in a position to hear a little on these matters rather than gain any
precise knowledge. I shall make this clear very quickly.
First of all, I shall go over what you said in the same
order. Then I shall demonstrate on what matters you
have been misled by ignorance of our ways. Finally I
shall destroy and refute all your reasoning. So, to begin
with my first point, you seemed to me on four—' 'Hush,'
said the Cardinal. 'To judge from your beginning, your
reply is going to be lengthy. So for the moment we shall
relieve you of the trouble of replying and keep it intact
for you for your next meeting. If you or Raphael here
has no other commitments, I should like that to take
place tomorrow.

" 'But meanwhile, Raphael, I should be very glad to
hear from you why you think that theft ought not to be

punished by death and what alternative penalty you suggest as being more to the public good. For not even you think that it ought to be tolerated. As things are now, men rush into theft despite the death penalty. Once you guarantee them their lives, what force or fear can restrain criminals? They would take the mitigation of the penalty as an inducement and invitation to crime.'

" 'Reverend father,' I said, 'it seems to me outrageously unjust to take away a man's life for taking money. For in my opinion human life is worth more than all the possessions fortune can give. But if they say that this penalty is aimed against the violation of justice and breaking the laws rather than the theft, would we not be right in calling this extreme justice extreme injustice? For we must not approve of legal ordinances so severe that the slightest disobedience is immediately met with a drawn sword; nor of decrees so stoical that all sins are considered equal, that it makes no difference whether you kill a man or steal money from him. If equity means anything, there is absolutely no similarity between these crimes. God has forbidden us to kill. Do we then kill so easily for the theft of a trifling sum? For if you interpret that commandment of God as forbidding killing except where human law declares a man ought to be killed, what is to prevent men from similarly deciding among themselves when it is permissible to commit fornication, adultery and perjury? God has forbidden us to kill not merely others but ourselves too. Now, if human agreement on mutual slaughter, on fixed conditions, has such validity that it releases its followers from that divine commandment and with no example from God allows them to kill people whom human sanction orders, are we not in this way giving only as much right to God's commandment as human law allows? And of course the result will be that in the same way men will decide in all matters how far it is convenient to observe God's commandments. The law of Moses, cruel and harsh though it was (for it was introduced against servants, and stubborn ones at that), yet punished theft with a fine, not death. Let us not imagine that in the new law of kindness, by which He rules us as a father his children, God has granted us a greater license for cruelty against one another.

" 'These are the reasons why I think it is not right. I am sure that everyone realizes how absurd it is and even dangerous for the state that a thief and murderer should be given the same punishment. For when a robber sees that no less a danger awaits a man condemned for theft than one convicted of homicide as well, by this single thought he is driven to murder the man he would otherwise merely have robbed. For if he is caught there is no more danger, and also there is greater safety in murder and a greater hope of concealing his crime if the witness is removed. So in trying to terrify thieves with excessive cruelty, we provoke them to kill good men.

" 'To turn to the question of what punishment could be more suitable, in my opinion this is much easier to find than a worse one. For why should we doubt that the profitable way for punishing crime is the one approved of long ago by the Romans, men who had great experience in governing a state? For men found guilty of serious crimes were condemned to be sent to the stone quarries or mines, and kept in chains constantly.

" 'Although in this connection nowhere have I seen a better institution than the one I noticed in my travels in Persia among the people called Polylerites. These people

are quite numerous and enjoy excellent institutions.
They are free and governed by their own laws except
that they pay an annual tribute to the King of Persia.
They are far from the sea, practically shut in by mountains, and enjoy the fruits of a bountiful land. They do
not visit others often, nor are they visited themselves. It
is an ancient practice of their country not to try to extend
their territory, and what they have is easily protected
from all attack by the mountains and the tribute they
pay to the powerful king. They are quite free from military service and lead a comfortable rather than a glorious
life, prosperous rather than noble or distinguished. For I
believe they are known to no one except their neighbors, even by name.

" 'In this country those convicted of theft return what
they stole to the owner, not to the king, as happens in
other places. For they think that the king has as little
right to the thing stolen as the thief himself. But if whatever is stolen cannot be recovered, the equivalent is paid
from the thieves' property, which otherwise remains intact for their wives and children. The thieves themselves
are condemned to hard labor. Unless the theft was a
violent one, they are not shut up in prison, nor do they
wear fetters, but they are free and unrestricted to do
their work for the state. Those who refuse to work or are
halfhearted about it, they flog rather than imprison.
Those who work hard suffer no violence and at night
merely have a roll call and are shut up in their rooms.
Apart from the constant work, there is nothing harsh
about their lives. For their fare is not too severe, and
as they are public servants, it comes out of public funds.
Some variations occur: in some places the funds to support them come from charity. Although this way is not

without risk, yet the people are so kindhearted that there is always plenty. In other parts some public revenues are marked out for that purpose. Elsewhere each man pays a tax for it. In several regions they do no public work, but any private citizen who needs laborers can hire their services in the marketplace for the day, at a fixed price which is slightly lower than what he would have paid for a free man. If such a servant is lazy he may be flogged.

" 'So they are never without work, and besides paying for their keep, this system also brings something into the public treasury every day from each of them. They are one and all dressed in the same color clothing; their hair is not shaved but cut a little above their ears, and a small piece is taken from the tip of one ear. Each man may receive food and drink from his friends and clothing of the proper color. But to give money is a capital offense for the giver as well as the receiver. No less dangerous is it for a free man also to receive money from a convict for any reason whatever, and also for a slave (this is the name they give to the convicts) to touch weapons. Each district distinguishes its slaves by a special badge, which it is a capital offense to throw away—just as it is for them to be seen outside their own region, or to have any conversation with a slave of another district. It is no safer to plan to run away than it is actually to do so. To be an accomplice in such a plan means death for a slave and servitude for a free man. There are rewards decreed for an informer—for a free man money, for a slave freedom. Both classes of such informers are given pardon and impunity if they were involved in the plan, to prevent its being safer to go through with it than to repent.

" 'I have shown you the law and arrangements dealing

with this question. It is perfectly obvious how humane and advantageous it is. The anger of the law takes the form of destroying the vices but saving the men, who are so treated that they must be good and spend the rest of their lives repairing the damage they previously did.

" 'So little fear is there of their falling back into their old ways, that travelers who have decided upon some journey think that the slaves are the safest of guides, and change them at each district. For if they want to commit robbery, they have everything against them: they have no weapons; money is merely an indication of crime; if they are caught, punishment is all ready for them; they have absolutely no hope of escaping anywhere. For how could a man conceal and hide his flight when his clothing is quite unlike everyone else's, except by escaping naked? Even if he did this, his ear would give him away. There is hardly any danger that they would enter a plot for conspiracy against the state. The only way for any district to entertain such hopes would be to win over the slaves of many other districts beforehand. But so far are they from being able to form a conspiracy, that they cannot even meet and talk together, or so much as exchange a greeting. Nor can it be imagined that they would fearlessly confide such a plan to their fellows, when they know that silence would be dangerous, but betrayal would be highly profitable. On the other hand, none is entirely without the hope that he may eventually recover his liberty by obedience and endurance and by showing that he is capable of leading a better life later. For every year several are freed as a reward for their patience.'

"After saying all this, I added that I saw no reason why this method should not be adopted in England too, with much greater profit than came from the justice the lawyer had so highly praised. At this the lawyer said, 'That plan could never be established in England without bringing the state into the greatest jeopardy.' While saying this, he shook his head, made a wry face and so fell silent. And all present gave their support to him.

"Then the Cardinal said, 'It is not easy to guess whether the plan would work or not without making an experiment. But suppose that after pronouncing the death sentence the King ordered a stay of execution and tried this method out (after abolishing all rights of sanctuary): if the plan worked out well, then it would be right to establish it permanently. If it did not, then those previously condemned could still be put to death. This would be no more against the interests of the state nor more unjust than if the execution were immediately carried out. Nor can any danger arise in the intervening period. I am quite sure that vagrants could well be treated in the same way. So far, in spite of all the legislation against them, we have achieved nothing.'

"After the Cardinal had finished, they all vied with one another to praise the suggestions that they had despised when they came from me—especially the point on vagrants, since this had been an addition of the Cardinal himself.

"Perhaps I ought not to repeat the absurd events that followed. Yet I will, as they were not bad and had some bearing on the subject.

"As it happened, there was standing nearby a parasite who wanted to seem to be playing the fool. But his imitation was quite lifelike. He tried for laughs with such feeble jokes that he was laughed at himself more often than his witticisms. Yet every now and then he brought out such a clever remark that it made us believe in the saying about dice: that eventually you are bound to throw two sixes. One of our company was saying that my suggestions had taken care of thieves and the Cardinal's of vagrants, and it now remained to give some public aid to people driven to poverty and rendered incapable of working for a living by sickness or age. The fool interrupted by saying, 'Allow me. I shall make good provision for this as well. For I should give anything to get rid of such people out of my sight. They have often made great nuisances of themselves by asking me for money with those whines and tears. But they have never been able to put them on successfully enough to get a penny out of me. For always one of two things happens: either I do not want to give, or else I just cannot, as I have nothing. And so they have now learned wisdom. For they do not waste their energy when they see me pass; they let me go by in silence. So they no longer have any hopes of getting anything from me, no more than if I were a priest. But I would pass a law to divide up all those beggars into the Benedictine monasteries and make them lay brothers and the women nuns.' The Cardinal smiled and applauded the joke, as the others genuinely did too.

"But a certain friar, who was a learned divine, was so amused by this witticism against priests and monks that he too began to joke, although normally he was a man of serious and grim appearance. 'No,' he said, 'you will not be rid of beggars so easily, if you do not also make some provision for us friars too.' 'And yet,' said the parasite, 'that is already taken care of. For the Cardinal made excellent provision for you when he decided that vagrants should be locked up and put to work. For you are the biggest vagrants of all.'

"When everyone saw that the Cardinal did not disapprove, they began to take the joke up eagerly, all except the friar. For it was not surprising that after being made the object of such bitter wit, his anger flared up so hotly that he could not restrain himself from open abuse. He called the man a knave, a slanderer, a backbiter and a son of perdition. All the time he cited terrible threats from the Holy Scriptures. Now the jester began to play the jester in earnest and he was a master in his field. 'Do not be angry, good brother,' he said. 'It is written: "In your patience ye shall win your souls."' Then the friar replied (for I shall repeat his actual words), 'I am not angry, you wretch, or at least I am not committing any sin. For the Psalmist says, "Stand in awe and sin not."'

"Then the friar was gently warned by the Cardinal to control his feelings. 'My lord,' said the friar, 'I am only speaking out of good zeal, as I ought. For the saints had good zeal and so it is said: "For the zeal of thine house hath eaten me up," and in church we sing: "The mockers of Elisha, while he went up to the house of God, felt the zeal of the bald"—just as perhaps he shall feel, that mocker, that ribald buffoon.' 'You are acting,' said the Cardinal, 'out of good feeling perhaps, but your action will probably be holier and certainly wiser if you do not get into a stupid quarrel with a foolish and stupid fellow.' 'No, my lord,' he said, 'I should not be acting more wisely. For Solomon himself, the wisest of men, says, "Answer a fool according to his folly," just as I am doing now, and I am showing him the pit into which he will fall if he does not take great care. For if the many mockers of Elisha, who was only one bald man, felt the zeal of the bald, how much more will it be felt by one mocker of many friars, among whom are many bald men? And we also have a papal bull, by which all who mock us are excommunicated.' When he saw that there was no end to this, the Cardinal dismissed the parasite with a nod, and gave the conversation a convenient turn to another subject. Shortly after this, he rose from the table and dismissed us, to give his attention to the cases of his clients.

"My dear More, look what a long story I have burdened you with! I should have been quite ashamed to keep on for so long if you had not eagerly requested this of me and seemed so intent on the tale that you did not want a single detail left out. For although I did so rather briefly, I simply had to relate it to show up the judgment of those fellows. For when they had despised my words, they began to approve of them when the Cardinal immediately showed his favor. They so fawned upon him that they even flattered and seriously entertained his parasite's ideas, when, as a joke, his master did not reject them. From this you can judge what worth the courtiers would put upon me and my suggestions."

"My dear Raphael," I said, "you have given me great pleasure by the wisdom and charm of all you said. At times I thought I was in my own country and even somehow to become a child again, by the delightful remembrance of the Cardinal, in whose palace I was brought up as a child. When you praise his memory so, Raphael, you cannot imagine how much dearer you are made to me on this account, although you were very dear even before. But I still cannot change my opinion in any way. I am quite convinced that if you could school yourself to tolerate princes' courts, you could do a great deal of public good by your advice. So there is nothing more appropriate to your duty, that is the duty of a good man.

Your Plato judges that states will become blessed only if philosophers become kings or kings philosophers. How distant will such blessings be if philosophers do not even condescend to give their advice to kings?" "They are not so ungrateful," he said. "They would gladly do so. In fact, they have already done this in many published books, if only those in power were ready to listen to good advice. But Plato was clearly quite right: if kings do not become philosophers themselves, they will never approve of the advice of philosophers, since from childhood they have been infected and tainted with wrong beliefs. Plato himself found this out in the case of Dionysius. If I were to put sound advice before some king and try to root out of him the pernicious seeds of evil, do you not think that I should be immediately thrown out or laughed to scorn?

"Now, suppose I were with the French King and sitting on his council in secret consultation, in a circle of wise men, with the King himself as president. The question earnestly being discussed is: By what means and wiles can he hold on to Milan, and drag that fugitive Naples back? After that, how can he overthrow the Venetians and bring the whole of Italy into subjection? Then conquer Flanders, Brabant, the whole of Burgundy, and other countries as well which he has already invaded in his imagination? Here one advises that a treaty ought to be made with the Venetians, to last only as long as suits the King's convenience; their plan should be shared with them; even a part of the booty be deposited with them, which he can get back when matters are finished to his satisfaction. Another urges that the Germans should be hired, another that the Swiss ought to be won over with money. Another thinks that the godhead of His

Imperial Majesty ought to be appeased with a sacrifice of gold. Yet another advises that peace should be made with the King of Aragon and that his own kingdom of Navarre should be given up to him as a guarantee of peace. Another is of the opinion that the King of Castile should be lured by some hope of affinity and some noble courtiers should be bribed to come over to their party. The biggest stumbling block of all is the question of England. But they agree that peace must be made and the alliance, always so feeble, should be bound with the strongest ties, so that they can be called friends and suspected as enemies. The Scots should be kept ready as if on watch, prepared for any opportunity, to be let loose immediately the English show any signs of activity. Some noble exile also should be trained secretly (for the treaties prevent this from happening openly) to maintain that the kingdom belongs to him so that the French King might have this weapon to check the king he suspects. Here, I say, amid such weighty discussion, with so many distinguished men vying to give their advice for war, suppose that all on my own I should arise and advise a different course: that Italy should be left alone and the French stay at home; that the kingdom of France is practically too big to be conveniently administered by one man, so that the King should not think of adding others. Then suppose I put before them the decrees of the Achorians, a people lying to the southeast of the island of Utopia. They once waged a war to obtain another kingdom for their king, which he claimed was his due inheritance because of some old affinity. When they finally won it, they saw that they had just as much trouble holding on to it as they had endured in gaining it. And seeds of rebellion were ever springing up within, or invasion from without. So they always had to fight either for the people they had conquered or against them. They never had an opportunity to dismiss their army and all the time their resources were being drained and their money going abroad. Their blood was being spent on others' glory and peace was no safer. At home characters had become corrupted by war, people had tasted the joy of robbery, boldness was strengthened by slaughter, the laws were held in contempt. The King, divided between the cares of two realms, could not give his proper attention to either. When they saw that there was no other end to these ills, at last they devised a plot and very gently gave their king the choice of retaining whichever kingdom he wanted. For they said he would not be able to have both and they were too numerous to be governed by half a king, since no one would willingly hire a muleteer to share with another. So that good king was compelled to give his new kingdom to one of his friends (who shortly after was thrown out) and be content with the old. Suppose that besides this I showed that after so many nations had been set in a turmoil for the French King's sake, when his coffers had been drained and his people ruined, by some chance these preparations for war would come to no purpose. I should tell him to look after the kingdom he inherited, and embellish it as much as he could, and make it as flourishing as possible; to love his people and be loved by them; to live together with them and make his rule gentle; to say good-bye to other kingdoms, since the one that had fallen to his lot was enough and more than enough. If I were to say all this, my dear More, how do you think it would be received?" "Not readily, I am sure," said I.

"Let us go on then," he said. "Suppose that his coun-

selors were debating with a king and devising means to
pile up money for him. One advises that the value of
money should be raised when the king has to pay any
out, and then lowered below its proper value when he
has to take any, so that he may pay much money with
little and receive much instead of little. Another advises
him to feign a war and on that pretext to gather in much
money; then, when it seems fit, to make peace with religious ceremonies to deceive the unfortunate people
who suppose that he is a holy king with compassion for
human blood. Another reminds him of certain ancient
moth-eaten laws, outdated by long disuse. As no one
remembers that they were passed, all have broken them.
So the king ought to impose fines for their transgression.
There could be no richer source, none more honorable,
since it wears the mask of justice. Another advises him to
forbid many things with heavy fines, especially such
things as are against the interest of the people; then to
give a dispensation for money to those whose interests
are damaged by the decree. In this way he would gain
favor with the people and profit in two ways: either
from the fines imposed on those whose greed for gain
has lured them into the snare, or else from the sale of
immunities, which, of course, will be all the more ex-
pensive in proportion to the king's goodness. For it is
only with the greatest reluctance that he allows any
citizen to do anything against the interests of the people,
and consequently only at a high price. Another recom-
mends that he should bring the judges over to his side to
give judgment for the king in every case; and that he
should also summon them to the palace and invite them
to discuss his affairs in his presence. In this way no case
of his will be so manifestly unjust as not to allow one of

them to find some crack in it for a false accusation—
either because he likes to make objections, or because
he hates agreeing with everyone, or else to win the king's
favor. Thus while the judges differ and a perfectly clear
case is disputed and the truth itself is questioned, the
king is given a convenient opportunity to interpret the
law to his own convenience. The others will support him
either from shame or from fear. So afterward their sentence is delivered from the bench without any fear. For
anyone pronouncing judgment for the king must have a
good excuse; for it is enough for him to have equity on
his side, or merely the words of a law, or the twisted
meaning of a document, or—what outweighs all laws
with conscientious judges—the king's indisputable prerogative. They all agree with that saying of Crassus: 'No
amount of money is enough for a king who has to keep an
army.' They all agree too that a king can do no wrong,
however much he may wish, since all men's possessions
are his and the men themselves too; that a subject owns
only as much as the king's kindness allows him to keep;
that it is greatly to the king's advantage that this should
be as little as possible, as he is safe only if his people do
not run riot with riches and freedom, since these are not
so ready to bear harsh and unjust commands; while on
the other hand, need and poverty blunt their spirits,
make them more patient, beat them down and take away
any brave hopes of rebellion. Suppose that in my turn I
should stand up and maintain that all this advice is both
dishonorable and disadvantageous for the king, since his
honor and safety rest upon the people's wealth more than
his own. I should show that they choose a king for themselves for their own sake, not his, so that by his toil and
care they may live profitably and safe from injury. So the

king ought to concern himself with his people's well-being rather than his own. It is just like the duty of a shepherd, who, insofar as he is a shepherd, must tend his sheep rather than himself. The very facts show how far wrong those people are who think that the people's poverty is a guarantee of peace. For where could you find more quarrels than among beggars? Who is more anxious for a change of government than a man who is discontent with the present condition of his life? Or who is bolder in stirring up revolution in the hope of gain from some source or other than the man who now has nothing to lose? If a king were so despised or so hated by his subjects that he could only keep them in their duty by outrageous measures, by plundering and appropriation, by reducing them to poverty, it would surely be better for him to abdicate than to retain his throne by measures by which he keeps the name of power but loses majesty. For it is not dignified for a king to exercise his power over beggars instead of rich and prosperous citizens. This was realized by Fabricius, a man of lofty and sublime spirit, when he replied that he preferred to rule the rich than be rich himself. And for one man to abound in pleasures and delights, while the others are groaning and weeping around him—this is to be the custodian not of a kingdom but of a prison. He is just like a bad doctor who can cure a disease only by bringing on another; for a king who can govern his subjects' lives only by taking away the comforts of life must admit that he does not know how to rule free men. He should change either his laziness or his pride. For it is mainly for these vices that his people despise or hate him. Let him live harmlessly out of his own pocket, fit his expenditure to his income, check ill-doing, by right training of his subjects prevent abuses rather than let them grow and then punish them. Let him not be quick to revive laws fallen into disuse, especially those which have been out of use for a long time and never missed. Nor let him ever, under the pretext of a fine, take anything which a judge would not allow a private citizen to receive, because it is unjust and cunning. Suppose I suggest to them the law of the Macarenses, who also are not too far from Utopia. On the day he ascends the throne, their king is bound, by an oath sanctioned by great sacrifices, that he will never at one time have over a thousand pounds of gold in his treasury or the equivalent weight of silver. They say that this law was introduced by an excellent king, who had more care for his country's well-being than his own wealth, as a bar to a king's piling up enough gold to create poverty among his people. For he realized that that amount would suffice, whether the king had to fight against rebels or the whole kingdom against an enemy's invasions. But it was not enough to incite him to invade other men's property. That was the main reason for passing the law. Another one was that he thought that provision was thereby made that there would be enough money in circulation for the citizens' daily trading. He also thought that since the king had to pay out whatever came into his treasury above the legal amount, he would not seek an occasion to do anyone an injustice. Such a king will be feared by the wicked and loved by the good. If then I were to put forward such suggestions to men violently inclined to the opposite, how deaf do you think they would be to my tale?"

"Very deaf indeed," I said. "Nor am I at all surprised, nor (to tell the truth) do I think that suggestions ought to be made or advice proffered which you are sure will never be taken. For how could so strange a tale do any good or work its way into their hearts, when the opposite belief is already firmly planted in their minds? This scholastic philosophy is all right among friends in familiar conversation."

"That is precisely what I meant," he said, "when I said that there is no place for philosophy with kings." "No, there certainly is not," said I, "for this scholastic philosophy which thinks that everything is appropriate everywhere. But there is another philosophy of a more civil kind, which knows the stage it should act on, adapts itself accordingly in the play it has in hand and plays its part appropriately and with decorum. This is the one you should adopt. Otherwise, when a play of Plautus is being acted, and the servants are trifling among themselves, if you come on stage dressed like a philosopher and recite the passage from the *Octavia* where Seneca disputes with Nero, would it not have been better to act a dumb show than by reciting inappropriate lines to make it a tragicomedy? For you would ruin and destroy the present play if you mixed in alien matter, even if the lines you brought were better. Whatever play is in hand, act it to the best of your ability, and do not wreck the whole of it because you remember another that is wittier.

"It is exactly the same in a state and the consultations of kings. If erroneous beliefs cannot be plucked out root and all, if you cannot heal long established evils to your satisfaction, you must not therefore desert the state and abandon the ship in a storm, because you cannot check the winds. Nor should you force upon people strange and unaccustomed discourses which you know will have no weight with them in their opposite beliefs. But you should try and strive obliquely to settle everything as best you may, and what you cannot turn to good, you should make as little evil as possible. For it is not possible for everything to be good unless all men are good, and I do not expect that that will come about for many years."

"The only result of this course," he said, "would be to make me as mad as the people whose insanity I am trying to cure. For if I want to speak the truth, this is what I must say. But whether it is appropriate for a philosopher to lie, I do not know. It certainly is not for me. Yet although my conversation might perhaps be unpleasant and annoying to them, I do not see why it ought to be outrageously strange. Suppose I were to say what Plato invents in his *Republic* or what the Utopians do in theirs—although this might be better (as I am sure it is), yet it might seem out of place. For in our society every man has his private possessions, but there everything is held in common.

"Admittedly my discourse cannot please those who have decided to rush headlong by the opposite road, since it calls them back and points out the dangers. But otherwise what else did it contain which could not, or indeed ought not, to be said anywhere? For if we ought to omit everything, as being strange and inappropriate, which the corrupt ways of men have made appear odd, then we ought to cover up among Christians practically everything that Christ taught and so strongly forbade us to cover up that whatever He whispered in the ears of His disciples He ordered them to proclaim upon the house-tops. The greater part of His teaching is much further removed from men's ways than my speech was. But cunning preachers, following your advice, I suppose, because men were loath to adapt their ways to the rule of Christ, fitted His teaching to their ways like a lead rule, so that at least they should join together somehow. I do not see what they have achieved by this, except that men may be evil with more safety. And I myself, I am sure, should achieve just as little in the councils of kings. For either I should be of a different opinion, which would be the same as having no opinion, or else I should be of the same and be a helper of their madness, as Micio says in Terence. For I cannot see the point of that oblique way of yours, by which you think that if everything cannot be made good, I should strive at least to get it managed suitably and rendered as little evil as possible. For with a king there is no place for dissimulation or conniving. One must openly praise the vilest plans and put one's signature to the most disastrous decrees. He would be considered a spy and almost a traitor who gave faint praise to wicked decisions.

"Moreover, nothing happens in which you could be of any benefit, when you are put amid colleagues who would more easily corrupt even the best of men than be corrected themselves, by whose evil company either you will be depraved, or else, in your blameless and innocent state, you will act as a cloak to another's wickedness and folly. So far from possible is it to change anything for the better by that oblique path.

"For this reason Plato shows with a beautiful comparison why wise men rightly keep away from politics. When they see the people swarm in the streets and get drenched with constant rain, and they cannot persuade them to move out of the rain and go to their houses, they know that they would achieve nothing by going out themselves, except to get wet with them, and so they keep themselves indoors. Since they cannot cure the folly of others, they are content if at least they are safe themselves.

"Although, my dear More, to speak the truth as it comes to mind, I think that wherever there are private possessions, where everything is measured by money, there a state can scarcely ever be justly and successfully managed—unless you think that is justice where all the best things come to the worst men, or that is success where everything is divided among a very few. Nor are they entirely prosperous, while the others are absolutely wretched.

"So I think over the wise and holy customs of the Utopians, who need so few laws for government so successful that virtue has its reward, and yet with equality of wealth all men have everything in abundance. Then I compare and contrast with their ways so many other nations, always making laws, but none of them all ever well enough governed, in which what each man gets he calls his own private possession. Their countless laws, passed every day, are not enough to help each man to obtain that which everyone calls his own, nor to protect it, nor to distinguish it from another's. This is clearly shown by those innumerable lawsuits which spring up all the time, but never come to an end. When I ponder on all this, I sympathize more with Plato and I am less surprised that he refused to pass any laws for men who refused those by which everyone shared all property equally. For that wise man saw that the one and only path to public safety lay in equality of property. I do not think that this could ever come about where each man has his own possessions. For where each man by fixed titles appropriates as much as he can, a few share out all the wealth and leave poverty for the rest. It usually happens that the one class of men deserves the lot of the other. For the rich are greedy, wicked and useless, while the poor are modest and simple men, and by their daily labor contribute to the public good rather than their own.

"So I am quite convinced that things cannot be distributed in equity and justice, nor mortals' affairs be managed prosperously, unless private ownership is totally abolished. If it is left, the greatest and best part of mankind will always have the worrying and unavoidable burden of poverty and cares. I admit that this can be somewhat relieved, but maintain that it cannot be eradicated. But suppose that it were decreed that no one should have above a certain amount of land, and that each man could only have so much money. Suppose that laws were passed to prevent excessive power in the king and excessive arrogance in his people; that it were decided that offices should not be canvassed or sold, and that no expense should be necessary for their tenure (otherwise an opportunity is given for repairing losses by trickery and plunder, and it is necessary to put rich men in charge of those posts which rather need the attention of the wise). By such laws, I say, just as desperately sick bodies can be supported by constant medication, so these evils too could be assuaged and lessened. But there is absolutely no hope that they may be cured and restored to a good condition, as long as private property exists. While you attend to the cure of one part, you make the wound in the other parts more inflamed. So from the cure of the one grows the disease of the other, since nothing can be added to one without being taken from another."

"But," said I, "I am of the opposite opinion, that life can never be comfortable with community of possessions.

For how could there be an abundant supply of things, when each man takes himself away from work? For considerations of his own profit do not urge him on, and confidence in another's industry makes him lazy. But when they are goaded by poverty and there is no law for a man to protect what he has gained, then must not constant murder and sedition vex the state? Above all, the authority of magistrates and their respect are abolished. I cannot even imagine what place there could be for such respect in men among whom there is no distinction." "I am not surprised," he said, "that you think this, when you have either no idea of what this would be like, or else a false one. But if you had been in Utopia with me and seen in person their habits and practices, as I did (for I lived there more than five years and would never have wanted to leave except to tell of that new world), then you would openly admit that this was the only place where you had seen a people properly governed."

"And yet," said Peter Giles, "you would have a hard time persuading me that a better governed people could be found in that new world than in this one known to us. For I think there are intellects just as good here and republics older than there, and long experience has discovered us many conveniences for life, not to mention certain chance discoveries of ours which no mind could ever have thought up."

"As far as concerns the oldness of republics," he said, "you could judge better if you had read the histories of that world. If they can be trusted, they had cities before we had men. Now, whatever up till now mind has discovered or chance found, could have come about in either place. But I am sure that although we excel them in brain, yet we are left far behind in enthusiasm and industry. For, as their annals show, before our arrival there, they had never heard anything of us (whom they call the Ultraequinoctials), except that once over twelve hundred years ago a ship was carried by a storm to the island of Utopia and wrecked there. Some Romans and Egyptians were cast up on the shore and stayed there ever after.

"See what use their industry made of this one opportunity. Every art within the Roman empire which could be of any use, they learned from the shipwrecked strangers or discovered from the basis they offered. Such profit did they take from the single arrival of people from our world. But if any like chance brought anyone here from their world long ago, this has been quite blotted out, just as perhaps future generations will forget that I was once there. As they from one encounter immediately made their own all our happiest discoveries, so I think it would be a long time before we adopted any of their better ideas. This I think is the most important reason why their state is governed more wisely and is more prosperous, although we are in no way inferior to them in intellect or wealth."

"So, my dear Raphael," I said, "I beg and beseech you to describe that island to us. Do not try to be brief, but unfold in due order their lands, rivers, cities, men, ways, institutes, laws—everything you think we wish to know. And you will think we wish to know everything of which we are so far ignorant." "There is nothing," he said, "I should be gladder to do, for I have it all ready. But it needs some leisure." "Let us go in then," I said, "to have lunch. Soon we shall take the time as we please." "Very well," said he. So we went in and had lunch.

After lunch we came back to the same place, and sat down on the same seat. The servants were told that no one should interrupt us, and Peter Giles and I urged Raphael to give us what he had promised. When he saw that we were anxious and eager to hear, he sat silent for a while, lost in thought, and then began in the following way.

BOOK TWO

CHAPTER ONE

On the Country and Its Agriculture

THE ISLAND of Utopia extends in the middle, where it is widest, for two hundred miles. For a great part it is not much narrower, but gradually narrows at both ends. This makes a circumference of five hundred miles and gives the whole island the shape of a new moon, whose horns are separated by about eleven miles of sea. The water opens up to a large width inside, and as the winds are checked by land on all sides, it is like a big lake, placid and calm. It makes practically all the bay there one big harbor, which is very busy and sends ships in all directions. The entrance is made dangerous by shallows and rocks. In about the middle of the gap a single rock sticks up, but it is not dangerous, as it is visible. They have built a tower on this to house a garrison. The other rocks are hidden and treacherous. The channels are known only to the Utopians themselves, and so it is not often that a stranger makes his way into this bay except with a Utopian pilot. For even the inhabitants themselves hardly have a safe entrance, except by marking their passage by certain signs on the shore. By moving these to different places they could easily lure an enemy fleet to destruction, however numerous it might be. On the other side of the island there are also many harbors. But everywhere the landing is so well protected, either naturally or artificially, that a few defenders could ward off great hordes.

But, as they tell and as the appearance of the place shows, that land was once not surrounded by water. It was previously called Abraxa and received its present name from its conqueror, Utopus. It was he who brought his rough and rude people to that high point of culture and civilization whereby they now surpass practically all other men. As soon as he landed and conquered the place, he caused that part where it was joined to the mainland to be cut through and let the sea around the land. He put to work on that task not merely the original inhabitants, but so that they should not take this work as an insult, he also joined to them all his own soldiers. With the labor divided among so many men, the task was completed with unbelievable speed. The neighboring people, who at the beginning had laughed at this idle undertaking, were struck with admiration and fear at the success.

The island has fifty-four cities, all of them large and magnificent. Their language, customs, institutions and laws are all the same. The layout of all the cities is the same, and, as far as the terrain allows, their appearance is the same everywhere. A distance of twenty-four miles separates the nearest cities, and none is so remote that a man cannot reach another in one day's journey.

From each city three experienced old men meet every year to discuss the common affairs of the island at Amaurote. This is considered the chief city, as it lies in the center of the island and is convenient for the representatives from all parts. The territories are assigned to the cities in such a way that in no direction does any one of them have less than twenty miles and in some directions they have much more—that is, on the side where cities are separated by a greater distance. No city is anxious to extend its territory. For they think themselves farmers rather than masters of what they have.

In the country throughout their land they have well arranged manors, well provided with farming equipment. The citizens take it in turns to live there. No country household has fewer than forty men and women, as well as two permanent slaves. In charge of all these are a man and wife of mature wisdom. Over each group of thirty households is put one phylarch. From each household twenty return to the city every year after completing two years in the country. In their place are put twenty fresh men from the city, and they are trained by those who have spent a year in the country and are therefore more skilled in farming. They themselves will teach others the following year. This is done in case their inexperience should harm the crops if they were all equally new and ignorant of farming. This practice of renewing the farmers is rigidly observed so that no one should be compelled against his will to endure the harder life any longer. Nevertheless, many who by nature love farming are allowed to stay on there. The farmers till the land, feed the animals, gather wood and transport it to the city by land or sea, whichever is more convenient. They rear a very large number of chicks, by an amazing device. For the hens do not sit on the eggs. Instead they keep a great number of eggs warm with an even heat, and so hatch them. As soon as the chicks come out of the eggs, they follow the men and recognize them as if they were their mothers.

They keep very few horses, and only high-spirited ones.

Their only purpose is to exercise their young men in riding. For all the work of plowing and carrying is undertaken by oxen. They admit that oxen are inferior to horses in power, but think they excel them in endurance and are liable to fewer diseases. In addition to this, oxen need less expenditure of effort and money for their keep, and finally, when their working days are over, they can be used as food.

They use grain only for bread. For they drink wine, cider or perry, or occasionally pure water, often also water in which they have boiled honey or licorice root, of which they have a large supply. When they have discovered (as they do very accurately) how much food is consumed by each city and the surrounding district, they yet plant a far greater crop and bring up far more cattle than their own needs require, and they share the surplus with their neighbors. They get from the city whatever supplies they need which are not kept in the country, and without any payment they get them from the city magistrates with no trouble at all. For each month several of them go to the city for a festival. When harvesttime draws near, the farmers' phylarchs report to the city magistrates how many citizens should be sent to them. This crowd of harvesters, arriving on the appointed day, can finish practically the whole work on one fair day.

CHAPTER TWO

On the Cities, and Especially Amaurote

WHOEVER KNOWS ONE of their cities knows them all. As far as the nature of the ground allows, they are absolutely identical. So I shall describe any one of them to you, as it does not much matter which. Which could be a better example than Amaurote? None deserves this more, as the others acknowledge it as head because of the presence of the Senate there, and none is better known to me, as I lived there for five years without a break.

Well now, Amaurote lies on a gentle slope of hill and is almost square in shape. Its side starts a little below the top of the hill and extends for two miles to the river Anyder. Along the riverbank it is somewhat longer.

The Anyder rises eighty miles above Amaurote from a small spring; but it is increased by the addition of other rivers, two of which are quite sizable, and before it reaches the city itself it is half a mile wide. Soon it becomes even wider and flows on for another sixty miles before entering the ocean. In all this distance that lies between the city and the sea, and also several miles above the city, the water ebbs and flows with a swift tide for six hours at a time. When the sea rushes in for thirty miles, it fills the whole basin of the Anyder with its own water and pushes back the river. And it contaminates the water with brine a little farther than that too; but above this the water bit by bit becomes fresh and when it flows past the city it is pure. When the tide recedes, the river follows it, pure and untainted almost to its very mouth.

The city is joined to the other bank with a bridge made not out of piles and timber, but out of fine stone arches. The bridge is in the part of the city farthest from the sea to allow ships to sail along all that side without any hindrance. They also have another small river, which is very calm and placid. It rises on the same hill the city is on and flows down right through the middle of it until it joins the Anyder. As the source of this stream lies a little outside the city, the Amaurotes have fenced it in and joined it to the city. This is done so that if ever they are attacked by an enemy, their water cannot be diverted or poisoned. The water is led off in brick channels in various directions to the lower parts of the city. If the ground prevents this anywhere, rainwater is collected in large tanks and is just as useful.

A high, thick wall surrounds the city, set with numerous towers and bastions. On three sides a moat surrounds the walls. This is dry, but deep and broad and entangled with briers. On the fourth side the river itself acts as a moat. The streets are well laid out for traffic and also to keep off the winds. The buildings are fine to see, as a long and unbroken row of them can be seen stretching along the whole street with their fronts facing you. These streets are twenty feet wide. At the backs of the houses for the whole length of the streets lie wide gardens, closed in on all sides by the backs of streets. Every house has its own door to the street and also a back door to the garden. These doors are made of two leaves;

they need only a slight push to open them, and close automatically. They let anyone enter and nothing is private anywhere. For they even change their houses by lot every ten years.

The gardens are very important to them. In them they have vines, fruits, herbs and flowers, all so neatly and carefully tended that I have never seen anything more prolific or more attractive. They are inspired to take this interest not merely because of the pleasure it gives, but by the rivalry between the streets for the excellence of their gardens. And certainly it would be hard to find anything in the whole city more profitable for the citizens or more pleasurable. It is for this reason that the founder seems to have paid more attention to the establishment of such gardens than to anything else.

For they say that the entire plan of the city right from the beginning was laid out by Utopus himself. But he left it to later generations to embellish and adorn it further, as he realized that this could hardly be done in a single life span. They keep records, written with great care and accuracy, covering the events of the 1,760 years from the conquest of the island. In these it is written that at first their houses were small, like cottages and huts, made out of any wood without discrimination; the walls were smeared with mud and the roofs rose to a ridge and were thatched. But now every house is remarkable for having three stories. The walls are faced with flint or plaster or brick, and are filled up with rubble. The roofs are flat and covered with an inexpensive substance so mixed that it cannot be harmed by fire and it is superior to lead for protection against the weather. They keep the wind out of their windows with glass, as it is quite plentiful there, or occasionally also with fine linen dipped in clear oil or amber. This dipping has two advantages, as by this means it lets in more light and less wind.

CHAPTER THREE

On the Magistrates

EVERY THIRTY HOUSEHOLDS each year choose a magistrate for themselves, whom in the older language they call a syphogrant and in the more modern a phylarch. Over ten syphogrants and their households there is an officer put in charge, previously called a tranibore, now a protophylarch.

The syphogrants are two hundred in number. They all swear to choose the man they think most suitable, and with a secret ballot elect a president, one of four previously nominated by the whole people. For one man is chosen from each quarter of the city to be put up for election before the Senate. The President holds his office for life, unless he is suspected of aiming at a dictatorship. They elect tranibores every year, but do not change them very often. All other offices are annual. The tranibores consult with the President every other day, occasionally more often if circumstances demand it. Their consultation is on matters of state and they quickly settle any disputes between private citizens, although these are very few.

They always elect two syphogrants to sit with them in the Senate, a different pair each day. It is sanctioned that no legislation affecting the state should be passed unless it has been debated for three days previously in the Senate. To make plans on public affairs outside the Senate or the public elections is an offense punishable by death. The reason for this, they say, is to make it difficult for the President and tranibores to conspire together to oppress the people with a dictatorship and so change the constitution. And so matters considered of great importance are put before the syphogrants for their vote. These report on it to their households, consult among themselves and then report their decision to the Senate. Occasionally a matter is brought before the council of the whole island.

The Senate has the practice of debating nothing on the first day it is proposed to them, but it is put off for a full meeting of their body. This is to prevent someone from babbling the first thing that comes into his head, and then from a perverse and unnatural fear of seeming to have been shortsighted in the beginning, thinking up arguments to defend his plan rather than consulting the interests of the state, ready to damage the public good rather than his own reputation. Such a man ought to have seen to it right from the first that he spoke with more deliberation than haste.

CHAPTER FOUR

On the Occupations of the Utopians

ALL THE MEN and women have one occupation in common—agriculture, in which everyone is skilled. They are all trained in this from childhood, partly by learning rules in school, and partly from being taken to the countryside near the city as if in play. As well as watching, they use the opportunity for exercise to gain some practical experience.

Besides agriculture (which, as I have said, is shared by all), each man is taught one occupation as his own specialty. This is usually weaving of wool or flax, or the craft of a mason, a smith, an ironworker or a carpenter. Nor is there any other trade there that occupies any number of men worth mentioning. For throughout the island there is only one style of clothing, except that one sex is distinguished from another and unmarried from married people by their dress. This style is retained all through life. It is attractive, allows easy movement and is designed to be equally suitable for cold and hot weather. Each household makes its own clothes. But of those other crafts each person learns one or another, not merely men, but women too. But because of their comparative weakness, the women do lighter tasks. They usually work wool or flax. To the men are assigned the

51

other, more laborious crafts. A person is generally trained to the craft of his father, as most men are naturally inclined that way. But if anyone's bent lies in a different direction, he is adopted into a household concerned with the craft he wants to practice. His father and the magistrates as well see to it that the new father he goes to is a worthy and honorable head of a family. If anyone learns one craft thoroughly and wishes to know another as well, he is likewise allowed. When he has a command of both, he practices whichever he wishes, unless the state happens to need one more than the other.

It is the chief and almost the only task of the syphogrants to see that no one is idle, but that everyone diligently sets about his craft, but not like a beast, worn out by constant toil from early morning until late at night. For even a slave is not as hard pressed as that. Nevertheless, this is the life of workmen practically everywhere except in Utopia. The Utopians divide night and day into twenty-four hours of equal length and assign only six to work: three before midday, after which they go to lunch; after lunch they have two hours in the afternoon for rest; after that they work for another three hours before dinner. Counting their first hour from midday, they go to bed around eight o'clock. Sleep claims eight hours. They are allowed to do as they please with the hours in between their work and sleep and meals. The purpose is not to allow them to waste this free time in wild living or idleness, but to enable them to apply their minds to whatever useful pursuit they wish in their free time. Most men devote their intervening hours to literature. For it is customary to hold public lectures every day before dawn. Only those are compelled to go who have been chosen by name to study literature. But a great number of men and women alike, from all classes, attend the lectures, their choice depending on their natural inclination. If anyone would prefer to spend this time in the practice of his trade (as happens to many who are not inspired by the thought of learning) he is not prevented. In fact, he is even praised as being beneficial to the state.

After dinner they devote one hour to games, in the gardens during the summer, and in the winter in the common halls where they eat. There they practice music, or refresh themselves with conversation. They do not even know dice and such foolish and pernicious games. But they play two games not unlike chess: one is a battle of numbers in which one number makes booty of another; the second is a game where, in battle array, vices fight with virtues. In this game a clever demonstration is given of the mutual discord of vices and their unity against virtues. It is also shown what vices oppose what virtues, with how much strength they openly assault, the wiles they use for oblique attack, the defenses virtues use to break the power of vices, the means they employ to foil their attempts and the ways in which either side gains victory.

But at this point, to avoid giving you a wrong impression, we must examine one aspect more closely. For as they spend only six hours in work, it might be that you think a shortage of supplies must follow. This is quite the reverse of the truth. In fact, this period of time is enough and more than enough to provide everything needed to support life or make it more comfortable. You will easily understand this if you remember how large a part of the population is idle in other countries. In the first place, there are all the women, a half of the total number; or if women are occupied in business anywhere, the men usually snore in their place. On top of this, there is a large and idle number of priests and religious, as they are called. Add to this all the rich men, especially the owners of estates, who are commonly called gentlemen, and the nobles. Add to these their servants, all that sewage of swashbuckling villains. Then count in the strong and healthy beggars, who use some sickness as a cloak for their laziness. You will certainly find that all these are far more numerous than the men whose labor provides all that human needs require. Of these latter, consider how few are engaged in necessary trades. For where we measure everything by money, many crafts are bound to be practiced which are quite useless and superfluous, merely the servants of luxury and vice. For if this large number now engaged in work were divided up to practice as few crafts as the convenient use of nature requires, then in the great abundance that would necessarily ensue, the prices would be too small to allow the craftsmen to earn a living. But take all those who now waste their time in idle occupations, and also all that mob enjoying the leisure of laziness and sloth, each one of whom consumes as much as two workmen who provide the goods; if they were all put to useful occupations, you can easily see how little time would amply suffice for supplying everything demanded by considerations of necessity or comfort, and of pleasure too if it is real and natural.

This is made clear by the state of affairs in Utopia. For there in the whole city and the surrounding neighborhood, scarcely five hundred persons of all the men and women strong and young enough to work are exempted. Among these are the syphogrants, who are legally released from work; but they do not use this privilege, so that by their example they may more easily attract people to their occupations. The same immunity is enjoyed by those to whom the people, persuaded by the recommendation of the priests and secret election of the syphogrants, give a perpetual release to allow them to devote themselves to learning. If any one of these falls short of the hopes entertained of him, he is thrust back among the workers. Contrariwise, it often happens that a mechanic spends his leisure time in such hard work on literature and makes such progress that he is taken from his trade and promoted to the class of scholars.

From this order are chosen ambassadors, priests, tranibores, and even the President himself, who is called in their old language Barzanes and in the newer one Ademus. Since the remainder of the population is neither idle nor engaged in useless trades, it is easy to estimate how few hours produce so much good work. In addition to what I have said, there is also this advantage: they have to spend less time in the necessary crafts than other people. For in the first place, building or repairing houses requires the constant work of so many men everywhere simply because a spendthrift heir allows the house his father built gradually to crumble. So his successor must at great cost begin all over again what could have been safeguarded for so little. It also often happens that a man fastidiously turns his nose up at a house that cost another a great deal. So it is neglected and soon falls down. Then he builds another elsewhere at no less a price. But in Utopia, where everything is in good order and the state well established, it happens only very infrequently that a new site is chosen for building. They quickly repair present faults and also take precautionary measures against those that are likely to arise. So the buildings last for a very long time with only a slight expenditure of labor, and workmen in that field occasionally have practically nothing to do—except that they are given timber to cut at home and stones to square and shape in the meanwhile, so that if any work does come it can rise more quickly.

Now see how few workmen they need for their clothing. When they are at work they are carelessly clothed in leather or skins, which will last seven years. When they go out of doors, they put a cloak on top to cover up their simple clothes. Throughout the whole island these cloaks are of the same natural color. So they need much less woolen cloth than is required in other countries and it also costs them much less. But linen is easier to produce and so is used more commonly. But in linen cloth only whiteness is observed, in woolen only cleanliness. No value is put upon a finer thread. Thus, while elsewhere four or five woolen cloaks of different colors are not enough for one man, and as many silk tunics, and for a more fastidious man not even ten are enough, in Utopia each man is content with one and it generally lasts him two years. For there is no reason why he should want more; if he obtained them, he would not be any better protected against the cold, nor would he seem one jot more attractive in his clothing.

So with everyone practicing useful crafts and fewer men needed for each, as there is a great abundance of supplies, occasionally they lead out a huge crowd to repair the public roads if any are worn away. Very often not even such work is required and so they make a public announcement of fewer working hours. For the magistrates do not exercise the citizens against their will in unnecessary work, since the institution of the republic has this one chief aim—that, as far as public necessity allows, all citizens should be given as much time as possible away from bodily service for the freedom and cultivation of the mind. For there, they think, lies happiness in life.

CHAPTER FIVE

On Their Lives Together

BUT NOW I must explain the interrelationships of the citizens, what mutual intercourse they have and what method there is for dividing everything up. Now, the city is composed of households and generally blood ties make up households. For when the women have matured, they are married and go to live in their husbands' homes. But male children and grandchildren remain in the household and obey the oldest of the parents, unless his mind is feeble from old age. Then the next in age takes his place.

Each city has six thousand such households, not counting the surrounding districts. To prevent the population from decreasing or expanding above the limit, no household is allowed to have fewer than ten or more than sixteen adults. No limit can be put upon the number of children. This number is easily maintained by transferring to smaller households those that are above the limit in larger ones. But if ever the number is exceeded for the whole city, they use the surplus to fill the gaps in their other cities. But if by any chance the numbers swell beyond the limit for the whole island, they choose citizens from any city and with their own laws set up a colony on the nearby mainland, wherever the inhabitants have too much land to cultivate. They take in any of the inhabitants of the country who wish to live with them. Thus joined with men who are willing, they easily merge into the same way of life and the same habits. That is advantageous for both peoples: for by their practices they bring it about that the land which appeared insufficient and niggardly to the others is now more than enough for both. But those who refuse to live by their laws they drive out of the boundaries they mark out for themselves. If they resist, they go to war against them. For they think it the justest reason for war when any nation refuses to others the use and possession of that land which it does not use itself, but owns in idle emptiness, when the others by the law of nature ought to be nourished from it. It is said to have happened only twice ever, from a plague, that some of their cities are so reduced in numbers that they cannot be replenished from other parts of the island if each city is to keep its level. In that case citizens return from a colony to make up the numbers. For they prefer their colonies to die out rather than let any of the cities in the island decrease.

But to come back to the common lives of the citizens, as I said, the oldest member is head of each household. Wives serve their husbands, children their parents, and, in short, the younger serve the elder. Each city is divided into four equal parts. In the middle of each pair is a marketplace for everything. There the produce of each household is brought and put in certain buildings. Each different kind of product is put separately into barns.

From these each family head seeks what he and his family need, and he carries off whatever he seeks, without any money or exchange of any kind. For why should anything be refused him? There is more than enough of everything and there is no fear that anyone will ask for more than he needs. For why would he be likely to seek too much, when he knows for certain that his needs will always be met? A man is made greedy and grasping either by the fear of need (a fear common to all creatures) or else (in man alone) by pride, which thinks it glorious to surpass others in superfluous show. This kind of vice has no place at all in the ways of the Utopians.

Next to the markets I have mentioned are provision markets, where they bring vegetables, fruits and bread, as well as fish and the animals and birds that can be eaten. These markets are outside the city where the filth and muck can be washed away in the river. From there they bring the animals that have been killed and cleaned by the hands of their slaves. For they do not allow their own citizens to grow accustomed to the slaughter of animals, as they think that constant practice in this gradually destroys the kindness and gentle feeling of our souls. Nor do they allow anything filthy and impure to be brought into the city, whose corruption could pollute the air and carry in some disease.

Moreover, each street has certain large halls set at an equal distance apart, each one known by a separate name. The syphogrants live in these. Thirty households, fifteen from either side, are assigned to each hall and take their meals there. The caterers of each hall go into the market at a fixed hour and after telling the number of their charges, get the food.

But chief consideration is given to the sick, who are

looked after in public hospitals. For they have four hospitals in the range of the city, a little outside the walls. These are so large that they could match as many small towns, and no number of patients, however great, would be cramped for lack of space. They also allow the isolation of patients who are suffering from a contagious disease. These hospitals are so well arranged, and so fully supplied with all things conducive to health, such tender and constant treatment is given, and the best doctors are so constantly in attendance, that while no one is sent there against his will, yet there is practically no one in the whole city who would not prefer to lie there when ill rather than at his own home. When the caterer for the sick has received the food in accordance with the doctor's prescription, then all the best remaining portions are divided equally among the halls, depending on the number in each. The only distinction is that some consideration is given to the President, the Bishop and the tranibores, and also to ambassadors and all foreigners—if there are any, as very rarely happens. These too, if there are any, are provided with certain houses properly equipped.

To these halls at the fixed hours of lunch and dinner comes the whole syphograntia, summoned by the sound of a bronze trumpet, except for those who are sick in the hospitals or at home. Yet no one is prevented, after the halls have had enough, from taking food home from the market. For they know that no one does it for no reason. Although there is no rule forbidding eating at home, yet no one does this willingly, since it is not considered honorable, and in any case it is foolish to take the pains to prepare an inferior meal, when a rich and plentiful one is to be had at a nearby hall. In this hall, the slaves do all the tasks that are dirty or burdensome. But the job of cooking and preparing the food and making ready the whole meal is left to the women alone, each household taking its turn. Depending on their number, the people sit at three or more tables. The men are placed near the wall, the women nearer the door, so that if any sudden illness comes upon them (as occasionally happens in pregnancy) they may get up without disturbing the company and find their way to the nurses.

These nurses sit apart with the suckling children in a room set aside especially for that purpose. There is always a fire and clean water and also cradles, so that they can put the children down to rest and, when they wish, take off their swaddling clothes in front of the fire and refresh them with play. Each mother is nurse to her own child, except where death or illness prevents this. When that happens, the wives of the syphogrants quickly find a nurse, and this is not difficult. For the women who can fulfill this function offer themselves to no task more willingly; since everyone praises this act of mercy and the child so brought up regards his nurse as his mother. In the nurses' room sit all the children under five years of age. All the other children of either sex who are below the age of marriage either serve at table or, if they are too young, stand nearby in absolute silence. Both classes of children eat what is offered to them by those at table, and they have no other set time for eating. The syphogrant and his wife sit in the middle of the first table, as this is the most distinguished place and from it can be seen the whole assembly, since this table runs across the highest part of the dining room. These are joined by two of the eldest present, as they sit four at a table. If there is a church located in that syphograntia, the priest and his wife sit with the syphogrant to preside. On each side sit the younger people and after them the older members, and so on throughout the whole hall. People of the same age sit together, but yet are mixed in with other age groups. They say that the reason for this practice is to allow the dignity and reverence of the old to check the young from unnecessary license in words and actions, since nothing can be done or said at table without being noticed by those nearby in one direction or another. The dishes are not served from the first place on, but first of all the older people, whose places are marked out in some special way, are given the choicest food; then the others are served impartially. If there are not enough tidbits to distribute to the whole company, the old people share theirs at their discretion with those sitting near them. In this way respect for the elderly is preserved and at the same time all have the same advantages.

They begin every lunch and dinner with some reading suitable for forming the character. This is kept short to avoid boredom. Using this as a basis, the old men indulge in moral conversation, which nevertheless is not gloomy or lacking in wit. But they do not occupy the whole meal with lengthy dissertations. Rather, they gladly listen to the younger members also and even deliberately provoke them to speak so that they may discover the nature and mind of each, as these betray themselves in the freedom of the table. Their lunches are rather brief, their dinners more lavish. For lunch is succeeded by work, but dinner by sleep and rest for the night. This, they think, is more conducive to a healthy digestion. No dinner passes without music, nor is the second course without its delights. They burn sweet-scented spices and scatter unguents and do everything to make the diners merrier. For they are readily inclined in this direction and think no kind of pleasure forbidden, as long as no inconvenience follows it.

In this way, then, they live together in the city. But in the country, as they are more widely scattered, they all eat in their own homes. For no household lacks for food, as they are the source of supply for the city.

CHAPTER SIX

On the Travels of the Utopians

BUT IF ANY of the Utopians wish to see their friends who live in another city, or to visit the place itself, they easily obtain permission from their syphogrants and tranibores, unless some special need keeps them at home. So there is sent with such men a number of people with a letter from the President showing that they have permission to be away and also fixing the day of their return. They are given a wagon with a public servant to drive the oxen and look after them. But if they have no woman in their company, they send the wagon back as a burden and hindrance. For the whole journey they carry nothing with them, yet lack nothing; for everywhere they are at home. If they stay in any place longer than one day, each man practices his craft there and is treated with great kindness by the workers in his craft. If anyone wanders beyond his territory on his own authority, and is caught without written permission from the President, he is treated with much abuse and dragged back as a runaway and punished severely. If he dares to do it a second time, the penalty is slavery.

But if anyone has the urge to wander through the territory of his own city, he is allowed to do so after obtaining the permission of his father and the consent of his wife. But into whatever country district he arrives, he is given no food until he has completed the amount of work normally done there before midday, or dinnertime, as the case may be. With this provision, a man may go wherever he likes within the territory of his own city. For he will be no less useful to the city than if he were actually in it.

Now you see how little freedom they have for being idle. There is no pretext for laziness, no wine taverns, no alehouses, no brothels, no occasion for vice, no lurking places, no secret meetings. Thus, under the watchful eyes of all, they must perform their usual work or enjoy honorable leisure.

As the people have this practice, an abundant supply of all things must inevitably follow. As this is equally distributed among all, no one can be a pauper or a beggar. In the Senate of Amaurote (which, as I have said, three men from each city attend every year), as soon as it is decided what product is in plentiful supply anywhere, or what is not so plentiful elsewhere, then immediately the abundance of one place makes up the need of the other. And this they do free, receiving nothing in exchange for what they give. But if they have given anything from their supplies to a particular city without asking for anything in exchange, they receive whatever they themselves need from another city to which they have given nothing. So the whole island is just like one household.

But after they have made sufficient provision for themselves (and this they do not think achieved until they have provided for two years, in case the next year's crop should be unsatisfactory), then from the surplus they export to other countries a great abundance of grain, honey, wool, timber, scarlet and purple dye, sheepskins, wax, tallow, leather and also animals. They make a gift of a seventh part of all these commodities to the needy in that country. By this trade they import into their own country not merely what they need at home (for that is practically nothing except iron), but also a great abundance of silver and gold. By constantly following this practice, they now have a great surplus of those metals, more than one could believe. And so now they do not care whether they sell for ready cash or on credit, having by far the greatest amount owed to them. In making these loans, they give no credit to private individuals, but rather to whole cities, with the usual documents drawn up. When the day for repayment comes, the other city gathers in the debts of the private debtors and puts the amount into its treasury; it then enjoys the interest on that money until the Utopians ask for it back. For the most part they never ask for it. For they think it unjust to take away from people who could use it, something for which they themselves have no use. But if circumstances demand that they should lend some part of that money to another country, then they ask for it back, or when they have to wage a war. For this single purpose they keep all the treasure they have at home, to protect them in extreme or sudden danger. They prefer to hire foreign soldiers for a huge wage, as they more willingly expose them to danger than their own citizens. For they realize that their very enemies can usually be bought by a huge sum of money, and either by treachery or civil strife be put in discord among themselves. For this reason they keep a treasury beyond value. Yet they keep it not as a treasury, but in a way I am really ashamed to relate, out of fear that my words will not be believed. My reticence is the more justified, as I realize that if I had not seen it in person, I could only with the greatest difficulty have been persuaded to believe the tale if told by another. For the less a thing fits the hearer's ways, the less credence is it always given. Yet a wise observer will perhaps be less surprised, since their other practices are so far removed from ours, if their use of silver and gold is suited to considerations of their ways rather than ours. For they do not use money, but save it for an eventuality which may or may not happen.

Meanwhile the gold and silver, of which money is made, no one of the Utopians values more than the nature of the things themselves deserves. In this respect, who does not see how vastly inferior they are to iron? Men could no more live without iron than without fire and water, though nature has given no use to gold and silver, which we might not easily go without, if man's folly had not put a price upon scarceness. Quite the reverse is truly the case: like a fond mother, nature has put all the best things in the open, like air, water and the earth itself, but has far removed empty and useless things. So if among the Utopians these metals were hidden away in some tower, the foolish cunning of people might suspect the President and Senate of tricking the people and getting some advantage themselves. Moreover, if they worked them into vessels and suchlike, if ever the occasion arose for melting them down again and paying them out as wages for the soldiers, they see, of course, that people

would be very annoyed at being deprived of things they
have come to enjoy as luxuries.

To remedy this, they have thought up a plan as har-
monious with their other practices as it is remote from
ours (as we value gold so highly and store it up so carefully). So only those who have observed it can readily
believe it. They eat and drink out of earthenware and
glass vessels, most elegant but yet cheap. But out of the
gold and silver, not merely in the common halls, but in
private houses too, they make chamberpots and all the
most humble utensils. In addition, from the same metals
they fashion the chains and thick fetters with which they
confine their slaves. Finally, those in ill repute for some
crime have gold rings hanging from their ears, gold rings
on their fingers, gold necklaces and gold headbands. So
they ensure in every way that in their country gold and
silver are in disgrace. So, although other nations feel the
removal of these metals as keenly as the removal of their
very entrails, yet no one in Utopia would think that he
had lost one penny if at any time circumstances demanded them all to be taken away.

They also gather pearls on the shore, and on certain
rocks diamonds and carbuncles. They do not go looking
for them, but if they happen to chance upon them they
polish them up. With these they adorn their young children. Although in early childhood they glory and delight
in such ornaments, yet when they have grown a little
older, without any warning from their parents, they observe that only children use such trifles, and then they
put them aside in shame. This is exactly like our children,
who, when they grow up, throw away their nuts, brooches
and dolls. These ways are so very different from other
nations', but how different are the mental attitudes they

produce, I never realized better than in the case of the ambassadors of the Anemolians.

These men came to Amaurote while I was there, and since they were coming to discuss important matters, those three citizens from each city had come before their arrival. All ambassadors from neighboring countries were in the habit of coming in the plainest possible clothing, since they had been there before and knew the character of the Utopians, and understood that they paid no honor to sumptuous raiment, despised silk and even rejected gold. But the Anemolians lived farther away and had had less intercourse with them. Upon hearing that all Utopians used the same rough kind of dress, they inferred that they just did not have what they did not use. So, with more pride than wisdom, they decided to deck themselves like gods in the elegance of their equipment, and to dazzle the eyes of the poor Utopians with the glitter of their finery. And so the three ambassadors made their entrance, with a hundred attendants, all in multicolored clothing, mostly of silk. The ambassadors themselves, being nobles at home, had gold clothes, huge necklaces and gold earrings, as well as gold rings on their hands and chains hanging from their hats, which sparkled with pearls and gems. In short, they were arrayed with all the things that in Utopia were the punishment of slaves, or the shame of people in disgrace, or the playthings of children. So it was worthwhile seeing how they preened themselves when they compared their ornaments with the Utopians' clothes. (For the people had poured out into the streets.) On the other hand, it was just as delightful to observe how wrong they had been in their hopes and expectations, and how far they were from producing the impression they had imagined. For all the splendor of their equipment seemed shameful to the eyes of all the Utopians, except a very few who had visited other countries for some worthy reason. They greeted the humblest members with reverence as if they were the masters, and considering the ambassadors themselves as slaves, because of their use of golden chains, passed them by with absolutely no mark of respect. You ought to have seen the children too! Those that had thrown away their gems and pearls, when they saw them on the ambassadors' hats, nudged their mothers and shouted to them, "Look, Mother! See that big booby still using his pearls and gems, just like a little boy!" But the mother, still taking it seriously, replied, "Hush, my son! He's one of the ambassadors' fools, I think." Others criticized those golden chains as being useless; for they were so thin that a slave could easily break them, yet so loose that he could shake them off whenever he wished to run away wherever he wanted, free and unfettered.

The ambassadors stayed there one or two days and observed that so much gold was thought so little of, and saw that it was despised there as much as it was honored in their own country. When they also learned that the chains and fetters of a single runaway slave took more gold and silver than all the trappings of the three of them, their feathers drooped and in shame they laid aside all that finery of which they had been so arrogantly proud. This came about especially after they had spoken more freely with the Utopians and learned their ways and opinions. For they are amazed that any man can be pleased with the feeble glow of a little gem or stone, when he can gaze at a star and the very sun itself; or that anyone is so crazy as to think himself more distinguished because of a thread of finer wool; for however fine a thread it may be, a sheep once wore it, and all the time it was nothing more than a sheep.

They are also amazed that gold, of its own nature so useless, is now everywhere so highly valued that man himself, through whom and for whose use it gained its worth, is valued much less than gold itself. This is so much so that some blockhead, with no more sense than a lump of wood and just as wicked as he is foolish, yet keeps many wise and good men in slavery, merely because he has a great pile of gold coins. If some chance or legal twist (which, no less than chance, exchanges high with low) transfers it from that master to the lowest wretch of all his household, soon he passes into the service of his servant, like an addition and tailpiece to his money. But much more are they amazed at and loathe the madness of men who pay practically divine honors to the rich, when they owe nothing to them, nor are they under any obligation to them, from no other consideration except their wealth; they do this even though they realize full well that they are so mean and greedy that, as long as the owners are alive, never will a penny come to them from such a huge pile of money.

They have formed these and similar opinions partly from their training, being brought up in a republic whose practices are very far removed from these kinds of stupidity, and partly from learning and literature. For although there are not many in each city who are exempt from other labors and are given over solely to learning (those, that is, in whom from childhood they have noticed an excellent character, an outstanding intellect and an inclination to good arts), yet all children are given a taste of literature; and a good part of the population, both men and women, throughout their lives spend those leisure hours we have mentioned in literature. They receive their learning in their own language. For it has a rich vocabulary, a pleasant sound and is an unsurpassed vehicle for expressing feelings. Practically the same language is current for a great area of that part of the world, except that it loses its purity outside Utopia in various ways.

Of all those philosophers whose names are so famous in the world known to us, not even a rumor had reached Utopia before our arrival. Yet in music and dialectic, in arithmetic and geometry, their ancient philosophers made practically the same discoveries as ours. But although they match our ancients in almost everything, yet they are far behind the discoveries of our modern dialecticians. For they have not discovered a single one of those rules which children learn everywhere in our world, about restrictions, amplifications and suppositions, all thought out with great acuteness in the handbooks on logic. Moreover, so far are they from finding "second intentions," that none of them could see Man Himself in the abstract, as they call it, although (as you know) he is absolutely colossal and bigger than any giant, and although at that time we pointed to him with our fingers. But they are very learned in the course of the stars and the motions of the heavenly spheres. They have even skillfully devised instruments of various shapes in which they contain very precisely the movements and positions of the sun and moon and the other stars which appear on their horizon. But they do not even dream of the "friendships" and "dissensions" of the planets and all that fraud of divination from the stars. They use certain signs seen long beforehand to forecast the rains, winds and other changes of the weather. But about the causes of all these things, and the tides and saltiness of the sea, and in general the origin and nature of the heavens and the earth, they partly put forward the same opinions as our old philosophers; partly also, as ours disagree among themselves, so they have different opinions from all of them, while they bring forward new explanations for things; nor yet do they agree everywhere among themselves.

In moral philosophy their discussions are the same as ours. They investigate the goods of the spirit and the body, and those of fortune; then whether the name "good" suits all these, or only those of the spirit. They discuss virtue and pleasure; but the first and foremost point of dispute is whether they think man's happiness lies in one thing or more. But on this point they seem to favor too much the side supporting pleasure, since by this they define the whole or the greatest part of human happiness. And what is more surprising, they seek support for so pleasure-loving an opinion from religion, despite its harsh, severe, sad and rigid nature. For they never discuss happiness without joining to rational philosophy some principles taken from religion. Without these principles, they think that reason in itself is maimed and weak for the investigation of true happiness. Their principles are such as these: the soul is immortal and by the kindness of God born to happiness; for our virtues and good deeds, rewards are appointed after this life, and for our sins, punishments. Although these tenets belong to religion, yet they think that men are led to believe and accept them by reason. If they are abolished, they claim without any hesitation that no one is so stupid as not to feel that he ought to seek pleasure by right or wrong means. This merely would he watch, that a lesser pleasure should not stand in the way of a greater, or that he should not follow a pleasure which would be rewarded by pain. For they consider it sheer madness to pursue harsh and difficult virtue, and not merely to renounce a pleasant life but even willingly to endure pain, from which you might expect no profit. For what profit can there be if you gain nothing after death when you have passed the whole of this life unpleasantly, that is to say, miserably. But actually they do not think that happiness lies in all pleasure, but only in that which is good and honorable. For to this, as if to the highest good, our nature is drawn by virtue itself, to which alone those of the opposite belief attribute happiness. For they define virtue as "living in accordance with nature," since for that purpose were we created by God. Whoever obeys reason in desiring and avoiding anything is following the lead of nature. Moreover, reason primarily inflames men to the love and veneration of the divine majesty to whom we owe our existence and the possibility of attaining happiness. Secondly, it advises and urges us to lead a life with the least worry and the greatest joy, and also, in accordance with the kinship of nature, to offer ourselves as helpers to all others to attain that same end. For never has there been anyone so stern and severe a follower of virtue and hater of pleasure, a man to enjoin labors, vigils and penance upon you, who did not at the same time bid you exert all your efforts toward lightening the need and discomfort of others and who did not judge that in the name of humanity what is most deserving of praise is that a man should save and console another. For it is a most humane virtue, and none is more appropriate for a man than to lessen the misery of others, remove the anguish of their lives and restore them

to joy, in other words, to pleasure. Why then should
not nature urge a man to do the same for himself?

For there are two possibilities: either a life of joy, that
is to say, pleasure, is evil, in which case you ought not
to help anyone toward it, but rather deprive all men of
it as far as you can, because of its harmful and deadly
quality; or else, if you are not merely allowed but even
commanded to win it for others as being something good,
why can you not do this for yourself above all others?
For it is only right to be as kind to yourself as to others.
For when nature encourages you to be good to others,
she does not then order you to be cruel and harsh to
yourself. So, they say, the life of joy, that is, of pleasure,
is prescribed to us by nature herself as the end of all
our activities. They define virtue as living according to
nature's prescription. But when nature encourages mankind to help one another to a happier life (and this she
does with good reason; for no one is so far above the lot
of the human race as to be nature's sole concern; for she
looks after all men alike, whom she embraces with the
common bond of similar appearance), you can be sure
that she repeatedly exhorts you to see to it that you do
not follow your own advantages to the extent of producing disadvantages for others.

Therefore they think that not only private agreements
should be observed, but also public laws. For either a
good president justly enacted them, or else the people
as a whole, not being oppressed by a tyrant or ensnared
by guile, sanctioned them by common agreement for
sharing the advantages of life, that is to say, the material
of pleasure. Provided that you do not violate these laws,
it is a mark of wisdom to procure your own advantage,
just as it is a mark of natural affection to procure that

of the state as a whole. But to deprive another of his pleasure while you achieve your own—this is injustice. On the other hand, to deprive yourself of something to give it to others is a task of humanity and kindness; this never removes as much advantage as it restores. For it is compensated by the return of benefits, and also the very consciousness of having done a kindness, and the remembrance of the affection and goodwill of those to whom you have been kind, bring on pleasure to the mind much greater than the bodily pleasure would have been from which you abstained. Finally, as religion is easily able to persuade a mind which readily agrees, in the place of a brief and small pleasure God repays us with a great joy which will never die. Therefore in this way, after carefully examining and considering the matter, they think that all our actions, and among them the virtues themselves, look toward pleasure as their final state and happiness.

By "pleasure" they mean every motion and state of the body or mind in which, with nature's guidance, it is pleasant to be. To this they add, with good reason, the appetite of nature. For not merely the senses, but correct reason also follows whatever is pleasant by nature, provided that the way to it does not involve injustice, the loss of a greater pleasure, or hard work as an inevitable consequence. But what men contrary to nature imagine by idle agreement to be pleasant for them, as if it were in their power to change things just as they do their names—all these things the Utopians decree are of no use for the attainment of happiness. Instead, these practices even hinder it greatly, if it is only because when once they have settled in a man, they seize on all his mind with a false belief about pleasure and bring it about that there is no room anywhere for true and genuine delights. For there are many things which of their own nature contain no sweetness, and even on the whole a large share of bitterness; but by the perverse enticement of evil desires, they are not merely considered as the highest pleasures, but even counted among the chief reasons for life.

In this kind of spurious pleasure they include those people I mentioned before, who think themselves the better for wearing better clothes. On this point they are twice wrong. For they are just as mistaken in thinking their clothing better as they are in thinking this of themselves. For if you regard the use of a garment, why should finer wool be better than coarser? But yet those men, as if their superiority lay in their nature not their error, preen themselves and think that their value is increased in this way. And so, as if by right, they demand for their finer clothes a respect that they would not have dared hope for in cheaper attire, and if they are passed by and neglected they feel outraged.

But is it not part of the same ignorance to enjoy empty and useless honors? For what natural and true pleasure is brought by another's bared head or bent knees? Will this heal the pain in your own knees, or the frenzy in your own head? In this image of counterfeit pleasure, men enjoy sweet madness who flatter and applaud themselves in their belief in their nobility; for they happened to be born of ancestors whose wealth, above all in land, goes back many generations (for nobility is nothing else these days). They think themselves not in the slightest degree less noble even if their ancestors left them nothing of it at all, or if they themselves squandered what was left to them.

In this number they also include those who, as I said, are delighted with gems and precious stones, and who think that somehow they have become gods if they obtain an especially fine one, above all, one of the kind most highly valued by their own people at that particular time. For the same kinds of stones are not considered valuable by all people, nor at all times. But they buy them only if they are removed from their gold setting and displayed all alone. In fact, they will not buy them even under these circumstances unless the seller takes an oath and gives them a guarantee that the gem or stone is genuine; so careful are they that a counterfeit stone should not deceive their eyes into judging it real. But as far as sight is concerned, why should a fabricated stone give less pleasure when your eye cannot distinguish it from a real one? Each ought to have the same value for you as it does for a blind man. What of those people who guard excessive riches, not to get any advantage from the pile but merely to gaze at it? Do they get true pleasure, or are they not rather deceived by a false pleasure? Or what of those who, by an opposite failing, hide away gold that they will never use and perhaps not even see any more, and who, in their concern not to lose it, do in fact lose it? For what else is it when you return to the earth something that you have removed from your own use and perhaps that of all men too? And yet when you have hidden your treasure away, as if you were now free of all care, you jump for joy. Suppose someone stole it and you died ten years later in complete ignorance of the theft. During all those ten years of your life when the money was gone, what did it matter to you whether the money was stolen or still safe? You can be quite sure that in either way you got the same profit from it.

To these foolish pleasures they join those of gamblers
(whose madness they know by hearsay, not experience)
and hunters and hawkers. For, they say, what pleasure
does it bring to throw the dice on the board, when you
have done it so often that if there were any pleasure in
it, you could have become bored with the constant experience? Or what pleasure can there be, rather than
disgust, in hearing the barking and howling of dogs? Or
what greater experience of pleasure is there when a dog
chases a hare than when a dog chases a dog? For it is
the same action in each case. For if running pleases you,
there is running involved. But if you are held by the
hope of slaughter and the expectation of seeing something torn to pieces before your eyes, it ought rather to
move you to pity to see a little hare so weak, shy and
harmless torn apart by a powerful, fierce and cruel dog.
So the Utopians delegate this practice of hunting, as
something unworthy of free men, to butchers (which
trade, as I have said above, is carried on by slaves). For
they think that hunting is the lowest part of that trade,
while its other parts are both more useful and more
honorable, since they produce much more advantage
and kill animals merely out of necessity; while the hunter
seeks nothing but pleasure from the slaughter and dis-
membering of a poor little animal. They think that this
delight in seeing death arises in beasts too, either from
an innate spirit of cruelty or else because the constant
experience of so savage a pleasure turns into cruelty.
Therefore they unambiguously decide that although the
common crowd of men considers them pleasures, these
and innumerable such-like practices have nothing to do
with real pleasure, as there is nothing in them sweet by
nature. For they are not moved from this opinion even

though these practices stir the senses with delight and this appears to be the function of pleasure. The reason is not the inherent nature of the experience, but the corrupt habit of the men involved. From this fault they welcome the bitter for the sweet, just as pregnant women have a distorted sense of taste and think pitch and tallow sweeter than honey. Yet no man's judgment, corrupted by disease or habit, can change the nature of pleasure, any more than it can change that of anything else.

They make various divisions in the pleasures they call true. For they assign some to the mind and others to the body. To the mind they give intelligence and that joy which the contemplation of the truth produces. To this they add the sweet recollection of a life well led and the certain hope of future good. The pleasures of the body they divide into two categories. The first is that which affects the senses with a clear delight. This sometimes comes about by the renewal of those parts which our natural heat has dried up. For these are restored by food and drink. At other times it happens when those things are expelled of which our body has too great an abundance. This pleasure is produced when we empty our bowels, or have sexual intercourse, or else by rubbing or scratching relieve an itching in any part. But occasionally a pleasure arises that is not going to restore anything our limbs lack or remove anything they have in excess; yet it tickles, affects and attracts our senses with a clear feeling by some secret force—for example, the pleasure of music.

The second kind of bodily pleasure that they define is that which consists of a calm and balanced bodily condition; that is, each man's own bodily health interrupted by no ill. For if no pain assaults it, this state of health is delightful in itself, even if it is stirred by no external pleasure. For although it is less obvious and less clearly perceptible than the swelling desire of eating and drinking, yet nonetheless many men think this the greatest of pleasures. Almost all the Utopians claim that it is a great pleasure, the foundation and basis of all others; for even alone it can produce a calm and delightful state of life, but if it is removed there is no place left anywhere for any pleasure. For merely to be without pain they call insensibility, not pleasure, unless there is also present a state of health. The Utopians have long since rejected the opinion of those who thought that a stable and tranquil state of health (a question hotly debated among them) ought not to be considered a pleasure because its presence could not be felt except by some opposite emotion. But now they practically all agree on the opposite opinion that health must be considered a very special pleasure. For, they argue, since in sickness there is pain, the implacable enemy of pleasure, just as sickness is of health, why then should there not be pleasure in the placid state of good health? They do not think the question is affected if you say sickness *is* pain, or sickness *contains* pain. For the same effect is produced in either case. If health is a pleasure in itself, or if it necessarily produces pleasure (just as heat is produced by fire), then in either case a man who has constant good health must also have pleasure. Moreover, they say, when we eat, all that is happening is that health, which had begun to be impaired, is using food as an ally to fight against hunger. While health is gradually growing stronger, that very advance to its customary strength produces the pleasure, by which we are refreshed. So if health rejoices in the battle, will it not also be happy when it gains the victory? When it has at last successfully gained its former vigor (its only aim in the whole conflict), will it straightway become stupid, and not recognize and embrace its own goods? For they think the opinion that good health is not felt to be far from the truth. For, they argue, who when awake does not feel that he is healthy, except the man who is not? Who is afflicted by such stupor or lethargy as to say that health is not pleasant and delightful? But what is delight except pleasure under another name?

Therefore they embrace chiefly the pleasures of the mind, thinking them the most important of all. They say that the most special part of them comes from the practice of the virtues and the realization of living a good life. Of the bodily pleasures they give first place to health. For they think that the joy of eating and drink, and whatever produces the same kind of delight, ought to be sought, but only for the sake of health. For such things are not pleasant in themselves, but only insofar as they oppose the stealthy attack of sickness. So just as the wise man avoids illness instead of hoping for medicine, and vanquishes pains instead of looking for consolations, so it will be better for him not to need this kind of pleasure instead of feeling its gratification. If anyone thinks himself blessed because of this kind of pleasure, then he must admit that he would be most fortunate if he spent his life in perpetual hunger, thirst, itching, eating, drinking, scratching and rubbing. Who does not see how disgusting and even how wretched such a life would be? Surely these are the lowest of all pleasures, just as they are the least pure. For they are never present unless joined to the opposite pains. For with the pleasure of eating is joined hunger, and by a

very unequal law too. For the pain is more intense, as
well as more enduring, since it is produced before the
pleasure and is extinguished only when the pleasure
dies too.

So they think that pleasures of this kind ought not to
be highly valued, except insofar as they are necessary.
But they do delight in these pleasures and gratefully recognize the kindness of fond mother nature, who uses
the most alluring sweetness to entice her children to
what must of necessity be done so often. For how miserable life would be if we had to drive away these daily
illnesses of hunger and thirst with bitter drugs, like the
other sicknesses that attack us more rarely! But they
gladly take care of their appearance, their strength and
their suppleness as being the special delightful gifts of
nature. They also pursue, as the delightful seasoning of
life, those pleasures that come through the ears, eyes and
nostrils, which nature intended to be peculiar to man.
For there is no other kind of animal that looks up to the
beautiful appearance of the world, or is stirred by any
sweetness of smell, except for choosing food, or is able
to distinguish consonant or dissonant chords in music.
But in all pleasures the Utopians have this reservation:
that a lesser pleasure should not get in the way of a
greater, and that a pleasure should not eventually produce pain. This they think necessarily ensues if it is not
a worthy pleasure. But to despise physical beauty, to
wear away one's strength, to turn nimbleness to sloth, to
waste the body with fasting, to injure one's health and
reject the other delights of nature (except if a man ignores his own advantage, while eagerly winning that of
others or of the whole state, since in return for this toil
he expects a greater pleasure from God), to punish

oneself for the empty shadow of virtue, to no one's advantage, or to strive after greater fortitude for an adversity that may never come—all this they think is absolutely insane. It is the action of a mind at once cruel to itself and ungrateful to nature, all of whose kindness they reject, as if they scorned to owe her anything.

This is their opinion on virtue and pleasure. They think that human reason can find none truer, unless revealed religion inspires man with something more holy. Our time does not allow us to discuss whether they are right or wrong in this opinion, nor is it necessary to do so. For I have promised to tell you of their practices, not defend them.

But I am quite sure that whatever may be the status of their decisions, there is nowhere a more distinguished nation, nor a more prosperous republic. They are quick and nimble in body, with more strength than their height would suggest. Not that they are short. And although their soil is not fertile everywhere, nor their climate perfectly healthful, yet they so protect themselves against the weather by temperance in living, and make up the deficiencies of the soil by hard work so successfully, that nowhere in the world is there a greater production of grain and cattle, nowhere are men's bodies more lively and liable to fewer diseases. Of course, you can see them carefully attending to matters that farmers look after everywhere, so that by skill and hard work they can improve soil none too rich by nature. But you will also see the people pull up whole woods by the roots and transplant them elsewhere. In this they aim not to increase the production, but to make transportation easier, so that they can have timber nearer the sea, or the rivers, or the cities themselves. For it is less laborious to transport grain far over land than timber. The people are affable, witty, clever; they enjoy their leisure, but (when necessary) can endure physical labor well enough—although they do not go out of their way to look for it; they never tire of mental study.

When they heard from us about Greek literature and learning (for we did not think they would like much in Latin except the historians and poets), they were very anxious that we should explain and teach it all to them. So we began to lecture to them, at first more to show willingness than because we expected any profit would come of it. But when we had made some progress, their industry immediately made us realize that our efforts were not being wasted. For they began to imitate the Greek letters so easily, to pronounce the words so accurately, to commit things to memory so quickly and repeat them so exactly, that we were astounded, although most of them came from the company of the scholars, men of chosen intelligence and mature years, who were not merely fired with their own enthusiasm, but were also ordered by a decree of the Senate. So in less than three years there was nothing in Greek for them to learn. They were able to read the good authors without any stumbling (except where the text was faulty).

In my opinion, they absorbed that literature all the more easily because, in a way, it was not alien to them. For I suspect that the Utopians have their origins in Greece, since their language, in other respects much like Persian, retains some traces of Greek in the names of their cities and magistrates. When I was planning my fourth voyage, I put on board ship a fair supply of books as cargo, since I had decided to stay a long while. Of these I gave to the Utopians several works of Plato an^d

more of Aristotle; also Theophrastus' work *On Plants*,
but, I am sorry to say, this was imperfect in many pas-
sages. For while we were sailing, I did not take enough
care of this book and a monkey found it. In his play
and frolicking he tore out several pages from different
sections and ripped them up. Of the writers of grammar
they have only Lascaris; for I did not bring Theodorus
with me, nor any dictionary except Hesychius and
Dioscorides. They are very fond of the works of Plu-
tarch, and are also delighted with the wit and grace
of Lucian. Of the poets they have Aristophanes, Homer
and Euripides, as well as Sophocles in the small Aldine
edition; of the historians Thucydides and Herodotus, together with Herodian. On medicine, too, my companion
Tricius Apinatus had brought with him some minor
works of Hippocrates, and Galen's *Microtechne*, which
books they value very highly. For although they need
medicine least of all people, yet nowhere is it more
honored, since they count knowledge of medicine among
the most beautiful and useful parts of philosophy. When
by the help of this philosophy they search out the secrets
of nature, they think that, besides gaining a wonderful
pleasure from it, they also obtain the highest favor with
its Author and Designer. They think that like other de-
signers he has exposed the workings of this world to
the sight of man (whom alone He created with ability to
understand it), and therefore He is all the fonder of a
careful and exact investigator and admirer of His work,
than of a man who, like an animal without any mind,
ignores so great and wonderful a sight, remaining dull
and unmoved.

So from their reading the Utopians are amazingly
clever at discovering devices to help make life more

comfortable. But they owe two such pieces of knowledge to us, namely printing and papermaking. Yet their debt is not merely to us, but also to themselves to a large extent. For when we were showing them the printing of Aldus in paper books, and telling them about the material used in making paper and about the art of printing, just talking rather than explaining clearly (as none of us had precise knowledge of either process), yet they immediately worked it all out on their own with great skill. Although they previously wrote only on skin, bark or papyrus, now they immediately tried to make paper and print. At first they did not get very far, but by constantly experimenting they soon mastered both. They made so much progress that, if they had the manuscripts of Greek books, they would not lack for printed copies. But as it is, they have only what I have told you about. But what they have, they have printed and multiplied into many thousand copies.

If anyone visits their country who is commended by some great intellectual gift or a knowledge of many lands from constant travel (which is why our landing pleased them so much), he is welcomed with open arms. For they are glad to hear what is done in every land. But only rarely do people go there for trade. For what would they bring? Only iron, or gold and silver, and then everyone would rather carry this away with him. As for their own exports, the Utopians think it better to transport them themselves rather than have others come to fetch them. In this way they can examine different people more carefully and not lose their experience and skill on the sea.

CHAPTER SEVEN

On Slaves

For SLAVES they do not have men captured in war (unless they fought the war themselves), nor the children of slaves, nor anyone who could be bought as a slave in another country. Instead they have any of their own citizens who have been reduced to slavery for some offense, or the inhabitants of foreign cities who have been condemned to death for some crime they have committed. This latter class is by far the more common. For they take away many of these, sometimes for a small price, more often for nothing, just by asking for them. They keep this kind of slave not merely in constant labor, but also in chains. Their own people they treat more severely: they think they are the more hopeless and deserving of the harsher punishment, because after such an excellent training to virtue they still could not be restrained from crime.

There is another class of slaves, composed of poor overworked drudges from another country, who have deliberately chosen to be slaves in Utopia. These are decently treated, and handled with not much less kindness than Utopians, except that they have a little more work imposed on them as they are used to it. It does not often happen that one wishes to leave, but if he does, they do not hold him against his will, nor do they send him away empty-handed.

As I have said, they treat the sick with great kindness and leave nothing undone to restore their health, whether it is by drugs or by dieting. If anyone is suffering from an incurable disease, they console him by sitting with him, talking to him and supplying all the comforts they can. But if a disease is not merely beyond treatment, but also a constant source of pain and agony, the priests and magistrates remind him that he is not up to all the tasks of life, is troublesome to others and a burden to himself, and is now outliving his own death. Then they advise him not to resolve to feed that pestilence and sickness any longer, nor to hesitate to die, since life is a torment to him. They bid him to take good hope and release himself from that bitter life, as if from a prison or torture rack, or at least give his permission for others to remove him. They tell him that since he is going to put an end not to pleasure but to punishment, he would be well advised to do it; and since in that matter he is going to take the advice of priests, the interpreters of God, his action will also be pious and holy. Those who are persuaded by this either end their own lives by abstinence from food, or else are released from it while they are asleep, without any sensation of death. But they never remove anyone against his will, nor are they any the less considerate to him. It is considered honorable to yield to persuasion and die like this. But they think a man unworthy of burial or cremation who commits suicide without having a reason approved of by the priests and Senate. Instead, in great disgrace, he is flung unburied into some bog.

A woman does not marry before she is eighteen years old, and a man not until he is four years older than that.

If a man or woman is found guilty of secret lust before marriage, the offender is severely punished and both are forbidden to marry forever, unless the President pardons them and forgives their offense. But also the head of the household and his wife in whose home the shameful act was committed are held in great disgrace, on the grounds that they were remiss in their duty. The reason for the severe punishment of this crime is the realization that very few people would join in married love, in which they saw they had to spend all their lives with one person and endure all the consequent inconvenience, if they were not carefully restrained from random sexual relations.

Moreover, in choosing partners, they seriously and rigidly observe a ritual that to us seemed quite absurd and ridiculous. A respectable and honored matron shows the woman (whether she is a maiden or a widow) to her suitor in complete nakedness. And in turn some trustworthy man shows the suitor naked to the girl. When we were laughing at this custom as being a silly one and were finding fault with it, the Utopians expressed their surprise at the amazing stupidity of all other nations. For, they said, in a matter involving a trifling sum of money, like buying a horse, other people are so careful that they refuse to buy the horse, however uncovered he may be, if the saddle and harness are not taken off, in case there is a sore hidden under those coverings. But in choosing a wife (a matter which will bring pleasure or revulsion for the rest of one's life) they are so careless that, while the rest of her body is concealed by clothes, they judge the whole woman from a space of a few inches (for only her face is visible) and then marry her —not without a great danger of a bad match if anything offends their taste afterward. For not all men are wise enough to regard character only, and in the marriages of such wise men bodily endowments make a useful addition to the spiritual virtues. Naturally so foul a deformity can lie concealed under those clothes that it can quite alienate the mind from one's wife, when it is no longer possible he be bodily separated from her. If such a deformity should happen to come about after marriage, then each man must bear his lot. But there ought to be legal provision to prevent anyone from being caught by such guile before marriage. The Utopians had to be all the more cautious on this, as they are the only people in that world who are content with one wife, and marriage is not often dissolved for them except by death, unless the reason is adultery or some unendurable fault of character. If either husband or wife is afflicted in this way, the Senate gives permission to him or her to find another partner. The other partner forever lives a single life, in disgrace. But they in no way tolerate a man to divorce his wife, if she is blameless, just because some physical misfortune strikes her. For they think it cruel to abandon anyone in his hour of greater need, and believe that it will also breed great distrust in old age, which both brings sickness and is a sickness itself. But it sometimes happens that the characters of husband and wife are quite irreconcilable, and they both discover others with whom they hope they can live more pleasantly. So they separate by mutual consent and contract new marriages. But this cannot be done without the permission of the Senate, which allows divorces only after its members and their wives have carefully examined the case. It is not easy even then, as they know that a ready hope of new marriage is most disadvantageous for strengthening the love of husband and wife.

Adulterers are punished with the severest slavery. If both offenders were married, the injured parties, if they wish, may gain a divorce and marry each other. Otherwise they may marry anyone they want. But if the injured party remains in love with so ill-deserving a partner, he is not forbidden to enjoy his right of marriage, as long as he is willing to follow the convicted partner in his hard labor. It sometimes happens that the repentance of the one and the constant kindness of the other move the President to compassion and gain them freedom once more. But if such a person falls back into his criminal ways, he is put to death.

For other crimes there is no fixed punishment regulated by any law, but the Senate judges the severity or mildness of the offense and decides upon an appropriate punishment. Husbands chastise their wives and parents their children, unless they have committed so terrible a crime that its public punishment is beneficial to morality. But usually the most serious crimes are punished with slavery. For they think this just as unpleasant for the criminals and more profitable for the state than if they hurried to execute the guilty and do away with them immediately. For their work brings more profit than their death, and by their example they can deter others from similar offenses for a longer time. But if in this treatment they rebel and fight against authority, then they are slaughtered like wild beasts that no prison or chain can confine. Yet if they are patient, not absolutely all hope is taken away. If after being subdued by long misfortune they clearly show enough repentance to demonstrate that their sin is more displeasing to them than their punishment, then sometimes by the President's prerogative, sometimes by the vote of the people, their slavery is mitigated or altogether remitted. To have tried to commit adultery is no less dangerous than to have succeeded. For in the case of every crime, they judge a fixed and clearly aimed attempt to be the equivalent of the deed itself. Nor do they think it ought to be in his favor that he did not go all the way, since it was not his doing that he failed.

They take great delight in fools. Although it is considered shameful to do them any harm, yet it is permissible to get pleasure from their foolishness. For they think that this is very good for the fools themselves. If anyone is so stern and severe that he cannot laugh at any word or action of theirs, to his safekeeping they refuse to entrust a fool. For they are afraid that a man who finds no use and no amusement in a fool (and this is a fool's only advantage) will not look after him with sufficient kindness.

To mock a man who is deformed or crippled is considered disgusting and disgraceful, not to the man mocked, but to the mocker. For he stupidly reproaches as a failing something that the man could not possibly avoid. They think a person lazy and slothful who does not look after his natural beauty; but with them it is disgraceful arrogance to seek help from paint. For they know by experience how little husbands are attracted by their wives' beauty as compared with integrity and humility of character. For although some men are won by physical beauty alone, no one's affection is kept except by virtue and obedience.

They do not merely deter people from crimes by punishment; they also set up rewards to incite them to virtue. And so they put up statues in the marketplace to distinguished men and those who have been great benefactors to the state. This is done as a memorial to their benefactions, and also so that the glory of their ancestors may serve their descendants as a spur and incitement to virtue. Anyone who canvasses for an office is debarred from all promotion. They live together in love, as no magistrate is haughty or terrifying. They are called "fathers" and so do they act. Those who wish may pay them respect, as is only right, but this is not demanded of men against their will. Not even the President himself is distinguished by his clothing or by a crown. His only distinctive mark is a small sheaf of corn which he carries, just as the Bishop's is a wax candle carried before him.

They have very few laws, as people so trained do not need many. The chief criticism they bring against other people is that an infinite number of books of laws and commentaries is not enough. The Utopians think it most unjust that any men should be bound by laws that are either too numerous to read or too obscure for anyone to understand. Moreover, they exclude absolutely all lawyers since these plead cases with cunning and slyly dispute the laws. For they think it useful that each man should plead his own case and repeat to the judge what he would have told his counsel. In this way there will be less doubt and the truth can be elicited more easily, since the speaker has not been taught any deceit by his lawyer, and the judge can shrewdly weigh up each point and help simpler minds against the false accusations of the cunning. It is hard for this procedure to be observed in other countries amid such a mass of tangled laws. But in Utopia every man has a good knowledge of law. For, as I have said, the laws are very few, and they think that the bluntest interpretation is the best. All laws, they say, are passed with the sole reason of reminding each man of his duty; therefore a more subtle interpretation reminds fewer people, as only few can follow it; whereas a more straightforward and simple meaning of the laws is open to everyone. Otherwise, as far as the common people are concerned (and they are the most numerous and most in need of being reminded), you might just as well pass no law at all as pass one and then interpret it in a sense that no one could possibly discover except by a very keen mind and much debate. For the blunt judgment of the common man could never discover such an interpretation, nor does he have enough time, with his days spent in working for his living.

These virtues of the Utopians have incited their neighbors, who are free and under their own control (for the Utopians long ago freed many of them from tyranny), to take their magistrates from them, some every year, others for a period of five years. After they have completed their term of office, they escort them back with glory and honor, and take back fresh ones with them to their country. Now, these nations take an excellent and healthy care of their states. Since the safety or destruction of a state depends on the character of its magistrates, they could have made no wiser choice than men who are strangers in the land and could not be deflected from honesty by any bribe (since it would shortly be useless to them when they returned to their own country), nor influenced by favor or hatred toward anyone. If ever these two evils of bias and greed settle on the law courts, they immediately destroy all justice, the strongest sinew of the state. The Utopians call the people who fetch magistrates from them "allies," and the others to whom they have given aid they call "friends."

Other nations are in the habit of making treaties all the time, then breaking them and renewing them. But the Utopians make none at all. For what is the purpose of a treaty? they say. It is as if nature does not put enough love between man and man. If a man scorns nature, do you think he would care about words? They are led to this opinion particularly because in that part of the world the treaties and pacts of princes are not observed very faithfully. For in Europe, and especially those parts controlled by the faith and religion of Christ, the majesty of treaties is everywhere holy and unbreakable. This is partly because of the justice and goodness of the princes, partly because of the reverence and fear felt for the popes, who most religiously perform whatever they undertake and bid all other princes keep exactly to their promises, while those who seek to evade them they coerce with the severity of their pontifical censure. For they quite rightly think it most disgraceful if there is no faith in the treaties of men who are called by the special name of "faithful."

But in that new world, as far separated from us by the equator as by their way of life and character, there is no confidence in treaties. The more numerous and sacred are the rites tying the knot, the more quickly is it undone. They easily find some verbal quibble, and occasionally formulate treaties deliberately in ambiguous language, so that they can never be bound by firm ties without having some loophole for wriggling out of the treaty and their good faith at the same time. If they found that this cunning, or rather this fraud and deceit, had played a part in an agreement between private individuals, they would look angry and shout "Sacrilege! They deserve the gallows!" while all the time they pride themselves on having given the same advice to their princes. This makes all justice seem either a lowly and humble virtue, far below princely eminence, or else capable of two divisions: The one befits the common people, going on foot and crawling along the ground, unable to leap over barriers, restricted with many fetters. The other is the virtue of princes, more august than the popular kind and much freer, which is allowed to do anything it wants.

As I said, I think that the reason why the Utopians make no treaties lies in the character of the princes there who keep their treaties so badly. Perhaps they would change their opinion if they lived here. However, they think that even if they are scrupulously observed, yet it was bad that the habit of making treaties started in the first place. This is the reason why nations think themselves born enemies and adversaries, just as if there were no natural bond uniting two peoples separated merely by a hill or a stream. Consequently such people think it right to plot the other's destruction if no treaties stand in the way. Even when they have entered upon a treaty they imagine that no friendship has been formed, rather that they still have freedom to plunder as far as the treaty has not been carefully worded and contains no sufficiently precise clause to ban this. But the Utopians are of the contrary opinion, that no one must be considered an enemy who has done no harm, that the fellowship of nature acts as a treaty, and that a better and more powerful bond exists between men from kindness than from treaties, that is to say, from the spirit rather than from words.

CHAPTER EIGHT

On Warfare

THEY ABSOLUTELY DETEST war and battle as being quite beastly and employed by no kind of beast as constantly as man. Contrary to the custom of practically all nations, they think nothing as inglorious as the glory gained from war. The Utopians, both men and women, on fixed days give themselves to constant military training to keep themselves in practice for the time when war is necessary. Nevertheless, they do not deliberately look for war, except to protect their own territory, or to drive off an enemy who has invaded the land of their friends, or out of pity for a people oppressed by tyranny to free them with their own forces from the yoke and slavery of the tyrant, as they do out of compassion. Yet they give aid to their friends not always to allow them to defend themselves, but sometimes they help them pay back and avenge wrongs already done to them. But this they do only if they themselves are consulted while the matter is still fresh. If they approve of the cause and are satisfied that restitution has been demanded but not made, then they take the responsibility of waging war. They do not make this decision only when an enemy has come on a plundering expedition. Their response is much more violent when their friends' merchants in any country,

either under cover of unjust laws or by the misrepresenta-
tion of good laws, suffer an unjust accusation under the
name of justice. This was precisely the reason for the
war that the Utopians waged a little before our time on
behalf of the Nephelogetes against the Alaopolites. For
in the land of the Alaopolites some merchants of the
Nephelogetes had suffered injustice, as the Utopians
thought, under the guise of justice. To the power and
malice of both sides were added the support and aid of
neighboring countries too. The injustice, if such it was,
was avenged by so savage a war, that of the most flourishing nations some were shattered and others were severely
beaten, and these evils upon evils were finally ended by
the slavery and surrender of the Alaopolites. As the
Utopians were not fighting for themselves, by this surrender the Alaopolites came under the power of the
Nephelogetes, although they were in no way to be compared to the Alaopolites at the height of their power.

So keenly do the Utopians avenge wrongs done to their
friends even in money matters, although they are not so
quick about their own. If they themselves are ever
cheated and deprived of their goods, as long as there is
no physical violence, their anger merely takes the form
of abstaining from trade with that nation until satisfaction is given. This is not because they care less for their
own citizens than for their allies, but yet they are more
annoyed if their allies are cheated of money than if they
themselves suffer this. For their friends' merchants lose
their own private possessions and consequently suffer
greatly by the loss. But their own citizens lose nothing
except what belongs to the state and what was in great
abundance and excess at home. Otherwise it would not
have been sent abroad. Therefore no one feels the loss.

So they think it excessively cruel to avenge a loss by the deaths of many men, when none of them feels any disadvantage from that loss in his life or way of living. But if any of their citizens are maimed in any country or killed, whether that is done by public or private plan, they investigate the matter through envoys. Unless the offenders are handed over, they cannot be restrained from declaring war immediately. If the offenders are handed over, they are punished with death or slavery.

If they gain a bloody victory, they are not merely sorry but even ashamed, considering it folly to have paid too great a price for merchandise, no matter how precious it is. They are very proud if they can conquer and overcome the enemy by guile and deceit. For this they arrange a public triumph and erect a trophy as if a great battle had been won. Then they boast that they have behaved manfully and courageously when they gain a victory in the way possible to no other animal than man, that is, by strength of mind. For bodily strength is the weapon of bears, lions, boars, wolves, dogs and the other beasts. Although most of them surpass us in strength and ferocity, they are all inferior to us in intelligence and reason.

The Utopians have only one aim in war—to gain that object which would have prevented them from going to war if they had previously won it. Or, if circumstances prevent this, they exact so terrible a penalty from their enemy that fear restrains others from attempting the same. These are the objectives they have, and these they aim at first of all. Yet they are more concerned with avoiding danger than winning praise and glory. So, as soon as they have declared war, they have many proclamations set up secretly all at one time in the most conspicuous parts of the enemy territory, signed with their public seal. In these they promise huge rewards if anyone kills the enemy leader. Then they announce smaller, but not inconsiderable, rewards for the head of each man whose name is contained in that same notice. These are the people they consider responsible, after the leader, for the hostile action against them. Whatever reward they announce for a killer is doubled if he brings any of the proscribed to them alive. They also try to bring over the proscribed persons themselves to work against their former allies, by the same rewards with an additional promise of impunity.

Therefore their enemies soon come to suspect others, and are not faithful or trusting among themselves, but live in the greatest fear and danger. For it is well known that frequently a good part of the proscribed and, above all, the leader himself have been betrayed by those in whom they placed the greatest trust. So easily are men persuaded to any crime by gifts. The Utopians set no limit upon these gifts, but remembering the peril to which they are inciting others, they see to it that the greatness of the danger is compensated by the size of the recompense. Therefore they promise not merely great amounts of gold, but also estates with great returns to enjoy as their own forever in safe places among friends. They keep their promises most faithfully.

This way of bidding for and buying an enemy is held in bad repute by other nations, as being a cruel crime of a depraved mind. But the Utopians think it most praiseworthy and a mark of prudence, since they can rid themselves of great wars in this way without a single battle. They also consider it an act of mercy and compassion, since by the death of a few guilty persons they save the lives of many innocent who would have fallen in the fighting, on their own side and on their enemy's. They feel sorry for the common crowd of the enemy almost as much as their own, since they realize that they do not come to war of their own accord, but are driven to it by the madness of their leaders.

If no progress is made by these means, they sow and foster seeds of discord by bringing the leader's brother or one of the nobles to hope that he will win control of the country. If domestic factions fail, they stir up their enemy's neighbors and set them in conflict by digging up some old legal claim such as kings are never without. They promise support for the war and supply money plentifully, but their citizens sparingly. For they regard them as so precious and value them so highly that they would not willingly exchange any of their citizens for the enemy leader. But they pay out gold and silver lavishly, as this is the only purpose for which they keep them. For their lives would be no less comfortable even if they spent it all. In fact, besides their wealth in Utopia itself, they have unlimited treasure abroad, since, as I said before, very many nations are in their debt. So they hire soldiers from all lands and send them to the war, especially from the Zapoletes. This nation is five hundred miles distant from Utopia toward the east, and it is rough, wild and savage. They prefer forests and craggy mountains, where they were brought up. They are a hard people, able to endure heat, cold and toil, unacquainted with luxuries, not concerned with agriculture. They pay little attention to their houses and clothing, devoting their energies merely to raising cattle. They live mainly by hunting and plunder. They are a nation born only for war, eagerly seeking any opportunity to wage war, and gladly embracing it once it is found. They go out in great numbers and for a low price offer their services to anyone needing soldiers. They know only this one art of life—that by which death is sought. They fight bitterly and faithfully for those under whom they are serving. But they do not bind themselves for any fixed length of time. They take sides on the condition that on the next day they will side even with the enemy if they offer a greater wage. On the next day after that they come back again if lured by a slightly higher sum. It is only rarely that there is a war in which a good number of them is not in each army. So it happens every day that men joined by ties of blood, who lived in great concord when hired on the same side, shortly after are separated to different sides and clash in war. With great ferocity, forgetting their birth and friendship, they plunge their swords into one another. No other reason incites them to this mutual slaughter than the trifling sum of money paid to them by opposing leaders. They are so careful about this money that if only one penny is added to their daily wage they are quite ready to change sides. So quickly have they drunk in avarice. Yet it is no use to them. For what they earn by their blood they immediately squander in luxury, and this luxury itself is not of a very high quality.

This nation fights for the Utopians against anyone, since they are hired at a price that cannot be matched anywhere else. For just as they seek good men to use, so the Utopians seek these worst of men to abuse. When necessity demands, they incite them with great promises and expose them to the greatest dangers, from which usually a great part never return to claim their rewards. To those that are left they faithfully pay what they promised so that they will be inspired to similar acts of daring. Nor do they care how many of these they send to their death, as they believe that they would earn the deepest thanks of the human race if they could cleanse the earth of all the filth of a people so foul and wicked.

After these, they use the forces of the people on whose behalf they are taking up arms, then auxiliary squadrons of their other friends. Last of all they join to them their own citizens. One of them, a man of proved bravery, they put in charge of the whole army. They also create two substitutes for him. If he is safe, they are both without any office; but if he is captured or killed, one of them succeeds to his position by a sort of inheritance. If it is rendered necessary by the many fortunes of war, the third man succeeds him to prevent the army being thrown into confusion because of the danger of its leader. A levy is held from each city out of those who volunteer. For no one is thrust out into military service against his will. They are convinced that if anyone is timid by nature, besides being no use in action, he will also make his companions afraid. But if any war presses close to their own country, provided that they are physically fit, they mix such cowards with men of better quality and put them on board ship, or else position them at intervals along the walls, from which they have nowhere to flee. So their fear is overcome by their sense of shame in front of their own people, the presence of the enemy and the impossibility of flight. And often extreme necessity turns into bravery.

Just as none of them is dragged to war against his will, so they do not prevent women who wish from accompanying their husbands on service. In fact, they encourage them and urge them on with praise. The

women who go out are positioned each with her own
husband together in line of battle. Also each man is surrounded by his children and relatives, so that those whom
nature especially urges to supply help to one another may
be of mutual assistance nearby. A husband who returns
without his wife, or a wife without her husband, is held
in the greatest disgrace, as is a son who returns after
losing his father. So if the Utopians themselves come to
be engaged in close fighting, as long as the enemy stand
their ground, a long and bitter battle ensues, which is
decided only by absolute destruction. As I have said,
they try every means to avoid having to fight themselves,
as long as they can wage war through the agency of
mercenaries. But when they cannot help going into
battle, they are fearless in handling what they wisely
avoided as long as they could. They do not grow fierce
at the first encounter, but rather by delaying they
gradually gain their strength and become so resolute
that they can more quickly be killed than repulsed. For
that security of a livelihood that each has at home, and
the absence of all anxious care for their families (a worry
that breaks brave spirits everywhere), give them a nobility of spirit that disdains defeat. Their military training also gives them confidence. Finally, they are given
courage by their right beliefs with which they have been
filled from childhood by their training and the laws of
the state. With this courage they do not hold life so
cheap as to throw it away to no purpose, nor so outrageously dear as to cling to it greedily and shamefully
when honor persuades them to lay it down.

When the battle is at its height and raging on all sides,
a band of chosen young men sworn to one purpose makes
for the enemy leader. They openly attack him, as well as

creeping up on him stealthily. They aim at him from near and far, and assail him with a long, unbroken line, with fresh men constantly taking the place of those exhausted. If he does not flee, he rarely escapes death or being captured alive by his enemies. If the Utopians gain the victory themselves, they never follow it up with slaughter. For they prefer to capture those who flee rather than kill them. But they never give chase without leaving behind one line of troops in full array under their standards. They cling to this rule so firmly that, if they gain victory with their last line after being defeated in all other sections, they prefer to allow all the enemy to escape rather than throw their own ranks into confusion by giving chase. For they remember an experience that has been not infrequent with them: after the main body of their whole army had been defeated and crushed, the enemy were exultant at their victory and chased the fleeing troops in all different directions; a few of the Utopian reserves watching for their opportunities suddenly attacked the scattered and straggling enemy, who were careless from an unwarranted sense of security. So they changed the outcome of the whole battle, and by wresting so certain and undoubted a victory from their hands, though conquered they conquered the conquerors in turn.

It is not easy to say whether they are more cunning in setting ambushes or cautious in avoiding them. You would imagine they are getting ready to flee, when nothing is further from their minds. On the other hand, when they do plan flight, you would never suspect it was in their minds. For if they feel that they are being pressed too hard because of superior numbers or the unfavorable ground, then by night they shift camp in complete silence.

Or they use some stratagem to deceive the enemy. Or else by day they retreat so gradually, keeping such good order, that it is just as dangerous to attack them when they are retreating as when they are pressing hard. They fortify their camps most carefully with a very deep and wide ditch, and throw the earth so excavated on the inside. Nor do they use slaves for this work. The task is done by the hands of the soldiers themselves and the whole army is engaged in the work, with the exception of those who are on armed guard in front of the rampart for sudden attacks. With so many helpers, they finish the large and extensive fortifications more quickly than would ever be believed.

They use armor which is strong enough to take blows, yet is so suited to any movement or gesture that they do not feel its weight even when swimming. For right at the beginning of their military training they get used to swimming in full armor. For long-range weapons they have arrows, which the infantry and cavalry can dispatch with great force as well as accuracy. For short-range weapons they use not swords, but axes, which are deadly with their sharp edge or sheer weight, according as the users slice or merely strike. They are extremely clever at inventing engines of war. When they have made them they are most careful to hide them in case their discovery, before they are needed, might make them ridiculous rather than useful. In manufacturing them, their chief aim is to make them easy to transport and suitable for maneuvering.

When they have made a temporary truce with their enemies, they observe it so strictly that they do not break it even when provoked. They do not devastate the enemy's land or burn his crops. In fact, they are careful

not even to trample them down with the feet of their
soldiers or horses, as far as possible, since they believe
that the crops are growing for their own use. They never
harm an unarmed man, unless he is a spy. If a city sur-
renders to them they protect it. If they take one by storm,
they do not plunder it, but kill the men responsible for
hindering the surrender and reduce the other defenders
to slavery. They leave untouched all the civilian population. If they discover that anyone advocated surrender,
they give him a share of the property of the condemned.
They distribute the rest among the auxiliary troops. For
of the Utopians themselves no one takes any of the booty.

But when a war is finished, they charge their expenses
not to the friends on whose behalf they incurred them,
but to the vanquished. On this account they make them
pay partly in money, which they put aside for similar
military purposes, and partly in land in the territory of
the defeated country, to belong to the Utopians forever
and provide them with a considerable revenue. They
have revenues of this kind now in many countries. They
were obtained gradually for various reasons and have
grown to over seven hundred thousand ducats a year.
To these they send out some of their citizens as financial
agents, to live in great splendor in the foreign country
and play the part of millionaires. But yet there is plenty
left to be paid into the treasury, unless they prefer to
lend it to the country producing it. They often do this
as long as the others have need of it. It hardly ever happens that they ask for the whole amount back. They
assign part of these landed estates to the men who at the
Utopians' request undergo the kind of danger I described
previously. If any king takes up arms against them and
is ready to invade their territory, they immediately rush

to oppose him in full strength outside their boundaries. For they do not like to make war on their own soil, nor is any necessity great enough to compel them to let foreign auxiliaries into their own island.

CHAPTER NINE

On the Religions of the Utopians

THEY HAVE DIFFERENT religions not merely in the island but even in single cities. Some worship the sun as a god, others the moon or any of the planets. Some look up to a man, not only as a god but as the highest god, if he was famed for virtue or glory long ago. But by far the largest section of the population, and the wisest too, adheres to none of these beliefs, but thinks that there is a certain single divinity, unknown, eternal, boundless, inexplicable, beyond the understanding of the human mind, diffused through the whole of this universe in virtue, not bulk. They call him "the father." To this one divinity they attribute the beginnings, increases, advances, changes and ends of all things. They do not accord divine honors to anyone else.

Although all the others have different beliefs, yet they agree with them on this point: they believe that there is one Supreme Being who is responsible for the creation and protection of the universe. They all agree in calling him Mythra in their native tongue, but they disagree in having different conceptions of him. Each man thinks that whatever he considers the Supreme Power is that selfsame person to whose divinity and majesty alone all nations assign the sum of all things. But they are gradually departing from that multiplicity of superstitions and coming together to that one religion which reason judges to surpass all others. It is quite certain that the others would have disappeared long ago, except that when anyone planned to change his religion, whatever ill fortune occurred, he interpreted it in his terror not as a chance happening but as a sign from heaven, as if the power whose worship was being abandoned was punishing the wicked design against itself.

The Utopians heard from us the name of Christ, his teaching, his ways and his miracles, also the equally wonderful fortitude of the martyrs, whose blood willingly shed brought over so many countries to their beliefs in all parts of the world. You would not believe how readily they agreed to this, whether God was secretly inspiring them or our religion seemed closest to the belief most prevalent among them. Yet I believe they were also brought to this opinion because they heard that Christ favored communal living among his followers and that this was still the practice in real Christian communities. But whatever impelled them, many came over to our religion and were washed with the water of baptism.

There were four of us left, as two of our company had died, and unfortunately none of us was a priest. The Utopians were initiated in the other points of Christianity, but still were without those sacraments which in our world only priests can supply. Yet they understand and make this their most earnest prayer. In fact, they even debate heatedly among themselves whether one of their own number could be chosen to receive the order of priesthood without the sending of a Christian bishop. And certainly it seemed as if they were going to choose one. But they had not yet chosen him when I left. Those who do not believe in Christianity nevertheless deter no one from it, nor attack a man instructed in it, except that one of our company was punished in my presence. He had been recently baptized, and much against our advice was discoursing in public on the worship of Christ with more enthusiasm than wisdom. So fervent did he grow that he not only extolled our beliefs above others, but absolutely condemned all others. He called the beliefs profane and their adherents impious and sacrilegious, deserving to be punished with everlasting fire. When he had been speaking like this for some time, they arrested him, then prosecuted and convicted him not for scorning a religion but for stirring up discord among the people. The penalty was exile. For it is one of their oldest established laws that no one should be penalized for his religious beliefs.

For right at the beginning King Utopus had heard that before his arrival the inhabitants fought constantly among themselves on religious issues, and he had observed that the reason for his conquest was that all the different sects were in strife and so fought singly for their country. So after his victory he first of all passed a law that everyone should be allowed to follow whatever religion he pleased; that a man might attempt to bring others over to his religion only to the extent of offering reasons calmly and soberly, without destroying others bitterly if he could not gain his end by persuasion; that he should not use any force and should refrain from abuse. If anyone goes beyond the limit in religious dispute, he is punished by exile or slavery.

Utopus introduced this law not merely to preserve peace, which he saw completely overthrown by constant strife and inextinguishable hatred, but also because he thought that such an enactment would further the cause of religion. He was never rash enough to give any definite view on religion, as if he was not sure whether God, desiring various and manifold worship, gave different inspiration to different people. But he thought it arrogant and foolish to demand by violence and threats that your views should be accepted by everyone. Even if one alone were true and all others idle, he easily foresaw that, provided the matter is handled with wisdom and moderation, the force of truth must eventually arise and stand out; but if there is armed strife and confusion, since the worst men are the most stubborn, the best and most holy religion would be overthrown by the empty superstitions, like crops among thorns and weeds. So he left the whole matter undecided and left each man the liberty to believe what he wished. But he issued severe and careful restrictions against anyone's so falling away from the dignity of human nature as to believe that the soul dies with the body or that the world revolves by chance without divine providence. And therefore they believe that after this life vice is punished and virtue rewarded. If anyone takes the contrary view, they do not even count him as a human being, since he has lowered the sublime nature of his soul to the cheapness of a beast's body. Much less do they consider him a citizen, as he would not have the slightest respect for laws and customs if fear did not compel him. For who can doubt that if a man has no fear outside the laws, no hope beyond the body, he will try to evade by stealth or overthrow by violence the public laws of his country, while gratifying his private desires. So if a man is of this opinion, he is given no share in public office, is entrusted with no magistracy and is put in charge of no public administration. Therefore he is despised on all sides as having a lazy and mean nature. Yet they inflict no actual punishment upon him, as they are convinced that no man is capable of believing anything he chooses. Nor do they force him by threats to conceal his mind. They do not tolerate deceit and lies, but hold them in the greatest detestation as being nearest to fraud. But they do prevent him from discussing his opinion, although this applies only to dispute before the common people. For they not merely allow but even encourage him to have private discussion with the priests and worthy citizens, being convinced that that madness will eventually yield to reason.

There are others of no inconsiderable number who are not so prohibited, as their beliefs are not entirely devoid of reason and they themselves are not evil men. These hold to a widely different error in believing that dumb animals too have eternal souls, although they are not to be compared to ours in dignity nor are they born to equal felicity. For they all believe as a sure and certain fact that man will enjoy such happiness, that while bewailing sickness, they lament no one's death, unless they see anyone being dragged from life in sadness and against his will. This they consider a very bad omen, as if the soul has given up all hope from a guilty conscience and is afraid to leave because of some hidden foreboding of imminent punishment. They also think that a man's arrival will not be welcome to God, if he does not run willingly when summoned, but has to be dragged protesting and unwilling. So those who witness this kind of death are appalled and conduct his funeral in sad silence. After praying for God's mercy on his soul and beseeching Him to pardon his weakness out of His kindness, they cover the corpse with earth.

On the other hand, whoever departs this life eagerly, full of good hope, is mourned by no one. They accompany his funeral with singing, commending his soul to God with great affection. At last they burn the body with reverence rather than grief, and set up a stone on the spot engraved with the dead man's titles. When they return home they recall his character and achievements, and no part of his life is told more often or more gladly than his happy death. This recollection of goodness they think is a most effective spur to virtue for the living and a most acceptable reverence for the dead. They believe that the dead are present at conversations about themselves, although they are invisible to dull mortal eyes. For it would not be appropriate to the lot of the blessed to be deprived of the freedom to journey where they wish, and it would be ungrateful to have thrown away all desire to see their friends, who were bound to them during life by mutual love and charity. They imagine that in good men, this love (like the other blessings) is increased rather than diminished after death. So they believe that the dead move among the living, as witnesses of their words and deeds. Therefore they go about their tasks with more confidence, relying upon these overseers. The belief in the presence of their ancestors also keeps them from secret dishonesty.

They completely discountenance and laugh at augury and the other forms of divination springing from idle superstition, which are much in favor in other countries. But miracles, which arise by no natural agency, they respect as being the work and witness of the presence of God. They say that they have frequent miracles in their country, and on occasion, when important matters of state are in doubt, by public intercession and with absolute confidence they obtain and receive them.

They consider the contemplation and praise of nature an act of worship pleasing to God. But there are a good many people who, from their love of religion, ignore learning and are not concerned to acquire any knowledge, although they do not give themselves up to idleness. For they believe that future happiness after death is earned by work and kind actions to others. So some minister to the sick, others repair the roads, clean out ditches, mend bridges, dig up turf, sand or stones, fell trees and cut them up, transport wood, grain and other commodities to the cities in carts, and in both public and private life they act as servants and even more than slaves. For whatever task there is anywhere that is hard, difficult or filthy, which puts off others because of the toil, disgust or sheer impossibility, this they take entirely upon themselves with a willing and happy heart. They procure leisure for others, but spend their own lives in constant work and toil. However, they do not blame or rebuke the lives of others, nor praise their own. The lower they go in their servile work, the higher is the honor accorded to them by all.

Yet these people are divided into two sects. The first consists of those who do not marry and who keep away from sex, as well as from eating flesh, some of them from the meat of all living creatures. They absolutely renounce the pleasures of the present life as if they were harmful,

and give all their attention to those of the next life by
vigils and sweat, when in the meantime they are keen and
energetic with the hope of soon winning the life to come.
The other sect is just as desirous of work, but they prefer
marriage. They do not despise the solace it brings, and
believe that they owe a work to nature and children to
their country. They avoid no pleasure, provided that it
does not delay them in their work. They like the flesh of
four-footed beasts, if only because they think that this
food renders them stronger for any task. This sect the
Utopians judge wiser, while they think the other sect
more holy. They would laugh at them if they attempted
a rational defense of their preference for celibacy over
marriage and for the hard life over the easy. But since
they claim they are led to it by religion, they look up to
them and revere them. They have no more anxious concern than to avoid any forthright pronouncement on any
religion. So this is what the people are like to whom in
their own language they give the special name
"bouthrescas," which may be translated as "religious."

They have priests who are very saintly and hence very
few. For they do not have more than thirteen in each city,
with an equal number of churches, except when they go
to war. Then seven of them set out with the army and
in the meanwhile their places are filled with others. But
when they return, each takes up his old position. Those
who are above the requisite number, until they duly
succeed priests who die, are companions to the Bishop.
He is the head of them all. They are chosen by the people, just like the other magistrates, by secret ballot to
avoid party strife. When elected, they are consecrated
by the college of priests. These are in charge of divine
affairs, look after religious matters and act as moral

censors. It is considered a great disgrace for anyone to be summoned or rebuked by them for loose living.

Their function is to exhort and admonish, but it is for the President and the other magistrates to check and punish the guilty. However, the priests are allowed to excommunicate anyone they find to be shamefully wicked. This is the greatest punishment they can suffer. For they are afflicted with severe disgrace and are tortured by an inward terror of religion, fearing that even their bodies will not be safe for long. If they do not quickly profess their repentance to the priests, they are arrested and punished by the Senate for impiety.

The priests instruct the boys and youths, and a concern for morals and virtue comes before that for learning. For they are very careful to instill immediately into the tender and obedient minds of the children good beliefs which are useful for preserving the republic. When these beliefs have settled in them as children, they follow them throughout life and prove extremely useful for maintaining the condition of the republic, which can be destroyed only by vices, and these are born from wicked beliefs.

Women also may be priests, but more rarely than men, and even then only aged widows are chosen. The male priests have as wives the most distinguished ladies in the country. For among the Utopians no magistrate is given greater honor, so much so that even if the priests commit a crime, they are not brought before a court. They are left merely to God and themselves. For they do not think it right to touch them with mortal hand, however criminal they may be, since they have so especially been consecrated to God, as a kind of offering. It is easier for them to observe this custom, as there are so few priests and such care is taken in choosing them. It does not easily happen that a man degenerates to corruption and vice, when he was advanced as the most virtuous of good men to a position of such dignity, with regard to his virtue alone. Even if this did happen (as human nature is so changeable), yet as they are so few and have no power except honor, there would be no great fear for the public safety from them. They have priests so few and far between to prevent the dignity of the order, held in such veneration by them now, from becoming debased by sharing their honor with many. This is all the more so since they think it difficult to find many people good enough for that dignity. To bear this office it is not enough to have average goodness.

Nor are they honored more among their own people than in foreign countries. The following tale will make this clear and also explain its origin. For when their forces are engaged in battle, the priests kneel down a short distance away, dressed in their sacred robes. They hold up their hands to heaven and pray above all for peace and secondly for victory for their country, but a bloody victory for neither side. When the Utopians are winning, they rush into the line of battle and stop them from showing cruelty to the vanquished foe. For an enemy merely to have seen them and addressed them in person is enough to save his life. To touch their flowing robes protects his other possessions from all outrage of war. Therefore with all nations they have acquired such veneration and so much true majesty that frequently they win no less safety from the enemy for their own men than they had brought to the enemy from their own citizens. For it is well known that on occasion, when their own troops have been pushed back and matters have looked hopeless, with the Utopians in flight and the enemy rushing in to kill and plunder, the slaughter has been stopped by the intervention of the priests, the troops of both sides separated and peace settled and arranged on equal terms. There has never been any race so fierce, cruel and barbarous as not to consider the priests' persons sacrosanct and untouchable.

For feast days they have the first and last days of each month and year, dividing the year into months. They measure the months by the course of the moon and the year by the sun. In their own language they call the first days Cynemerns and the last days Trapemerns. These names mean "First Feast" and "Last Feast."

Their churches are wonderful to see. For they are not merely examples of excellent craftsmanship but, as was necessary because of the small number of churches, they can hold an immense number of people. But they are all fairly dark. They say this was done not from ignorance of how to build, but on the advice of the priests, as they think too much light scatters men's thoughts, while a darker, dim light gathers together the mind and increases devotion. Since religion is not the same for them all, and yet they all take the form, however varied and manifold they are, of coming by different ways to the goal of worship of the divine nature, therefore there is nothing seen or heard in their churches which would not fit them all alike. If any sect has its own special rite, each man performs it in his own home. The public rites they manage in such a way as to take nothing from the private.

Therefore no image of a god is seen in any church. So everyone is free to imagine God as he wishes according to his own religion. They have no special name for God except Mythra. By this name they all agree upon the single nature of a divine majesty, whatever it may be.

Only those prayers are used which anyone could utter without offending his particular sect.

So on the days of the Last Feasts they come together to church in the evening, still fasting, to give thanks to God for the successful completion of the month or year of which it is the last day. The following day is the First Feast. They flock to the churches in the morning to pray for a happy and successful outcome of the year or month they are beginning with that feast day. But on the Last Feasts, before they go to church, at home the wives kneel before their husbands, and children before their parents, and confess that they have sinned by some actual deed or else by some carelessness in their duty. They then beg forgiveness for their mistake. So if any cloud of discord has arisen at home, it is blown away by such atonement. So they take part in the services at church with a pure and peaceful mind. For it is an offense to be present with a troubled mind. For this reason, people do not go to the rites if they are aware of harboring anger or hatred against anyone, until they have become reconciled and purged their feelings, for fear of swift and great punishment.

When they come to church, the men sit on the right, and the women on their own on the left. They seat themselves so that the male members of each household sit in front of the head of the house and the females in front of his wife. In this way it is arranged that the gestures of every member in public are observed by those by whose authority and discipline they are controlled at home. They are also careful to see that a younger person is everywhere near an older, in case children put in the charge of other children should spend in childish frivolity the time in which they ought to be forming a religious fear toward God, a great and almost unique incitement to virtue.

They kill no animal in sacrifices, nor do they believe that the divine mercy delights in blood and slaughter. For He gave animals life that they might live. They burn incense and other sweet-smelling things. They also carry a large number of candles, not that they fail to realize that such things contribute no more to the divine nature than do men's prayers, but this harmless kind of worship pleases them. And by these scents and lights and the other ceremonies, men feel somehow that they are lifted up and rise to worship God with more fervent mind. In church the people wear white. The priest has many-colored robes, wonderful in workmanship and design, although the material is not very valuable. For they are not embroidered with gold or set with precious stones, but they are worked so cleverly and expertly from different feathers that no costly material could equal the value of the work. Moreover, in these birds' feathers and the definite arrangement they have in the priest's vestments, they say that there are contained certain mysteries. The priests zealously teach the interpretation of these feathers, and when it is known, people are reminded of God's goodness to them, the reverence they owe in turn to God, and their duties to one another.

When the priest first comes out of the vestry in these vestments, they all immediately fall to the floor in reverence. There is such profound silence on all sides that the very scene inspires a kind of fear as if some divinity were present. They lie like this for a little while, and at a sign from the priest they stand up. Then they sing God's praises to the accompaniment of musical instruments, which are mainly of a form different from that seen in our world. Most of them far exceed ours in sweetness, but yet some of them are not even to be compared with ours. But in one matter they are clearly far ahead of us. All their music, whether it is played on instruments or performed by the human voice, so imitates and represents natural feelings that the sound is adapted to the subject. Whether it is a prayer or a tune of gladness, peace, trouble, sadness or anger, it so reproduces the feeling by the form of the melody that it affects the listeners' minds in an amazing way, sinks into them and inflames their spirits.

At the end the priest and people together recite solemn prayers in a fixed form of words. These are so composed that what they all say together, each man may apply privately to himself. In these everyone recognizes God as the author of creation and guidance of the world, and of all good things as well. He thanks God for so many benefits received, but specifically that by God's kindness he chanced to be born in that most blessed republic and that he was taught that religion which he hopes is truest. It is his prayer that God's goodness will bring it to his knowledge if he is in any way wrong in this, and if there is anything better than his country and religion and more acceptable to God. For he is ready to follow, he says, wherever God leads him. But if this form of republic is best and his religion most correct, then he prays God to grant him steadfastness and to lead all other men to that way of life and to the same belief about God, unless there is anything in this variety of religions that pleases God's inscrutable will. Finally he prays that he may have an easy death before being received to Him—how soon or late he does not dare to suggest. Although, if this does not offend His majesty, he would much rather die a difficult death and come to God than be kept from Him any longer in the most prosperous of lives. After this prayer they again fall to the floor. Shortly afterward they stand up and go to lunch. The remainder of the day they pass in games and military exercises.

I have described to you as truthfully as I could the form of the republic which I judge not merely the best, but the only one that can rightfully claim the name of republic. For elsewhere men talk of public good, but look after their private good. In Utopia, where nothing is private, they really do public business. In both places there is good reason for acting as they do. For elsewhere, everyone knows that however prosperous the republic may be, he will starve of hunger if he does not make some separate provision for himself. And so he is forced to believe that he ought to take account of himself rather than the people, that is, others. On the other hand, in Utopia, where all possessions are in common, everyone is certain that, provided that care is taken to keep the public barns full, everyone will have whatever he wants for his private use. For there is no unfair distribution of property, there are no paupers or beggars there, and though no one has anything, yet all are rich. What greater riches can there be than a life in happiness and peace, with all cares removed, without being worried about one's own food, or being harassed by one's wife's complaints and demands, or being afraid of poverty for one's son or anxious about a daughter's dowry? Instead they are assured of the livelihood and happiness of themselves and all their family, wife, sons, grandchildren, great-grandchildren, great-great-grandchildren and all the long list of descendants that nobles assume. Care is also taken of people who are incapable of the work they once did, just as much as for those still able.

At this point I should like someone to dare to compare with this equity the justice of other nations. I'll be damned if I can find any trace of justice or equity among them. For what sort of justice is this when some noble or goldsmith or moneylender or any one of those who do either nothing or else nothing very necessary to the republic achieves a glorious and splendid life either by idleness or unnecessary business? Meanwhile a laborer, carter, smith or farmer suffers heavy and constant toil that beasts could hardly endure, work so necessary that no republic could last without it for even one year. Yet they provide so poor a living for themselves and lead such a miserable life that the condition of beasts might seem far preferable. For the animals do not suffer such constant toil, and their food is not much worse and is pleasanter to them, nor do they meanwhile have any fear for the future. But men are incited for the present by barren and unprofitable work, and killed off by the recollection of an impoverished old age. For as they do not earn enough each day to keep them for that day, they certainly cannot have any surplus to put away for their old age each day.

Is this not an unjust and ungrateful republic which lavishes such riches upon the nobles, as they call them, and the goldsmiths and the others of that kind, who are idlers or mere flatterers and inventors of empty pleasures? Yet it makes no kindly provision for farmers, coal miners, laborers, carters and smiths, without whom there would be no republic at all. The republic abuses their labor when they are young and healthy, but when they are slow with age and sickness and utterly destitute, she forgets the sleepless nights they have spent and does not remember their many great benefits. Instead she shows her ingratitude by rewarding them with a wretched death. On top of this, from the daily wage of the poor, the rich wear something away every day, not merely by private fraud but even by public laws. So while it previously seemed unjust to give unkindness in return for good service to the state, the rich have twisted this and by passing laws made it justice.

And so, when I examine and consider all the flourishing republics in the world today, believe me, nothing comes to mind except a conspiracy of the rich, who seek their own advantage under the name and title of the republic. They also devise and think up all sorts of ways and means to hold on to their ill-gotten gains with no fear of losing them, and then to hire the labor of all the poor at the lowest price and abuse them. When once the rich have decreed that these devices are to be observed in the public name (in other words, in the name of the poor too), they then become laws. But when vile men with their insatiable greed have shared among themselves what would have been enough for everybody, even so they are very far from the prosperity of the Utopian republic. Since all greed for money and also the use of it have been removed in Utopia, how great a burden of troubles has been cut back and how great a harvest of crimes has been torn up by the roots! For who does not realize that fraud, theft, plunder, quarrels, brawls, discord, sedition, murder, treachery, poisoning—all these are avenged by daily punishment, not checked; but if money is killed, they will die with it? Also fear, worry, care, toil and sleepless nights will also perish at the same moment as money. Yes, poverty itself, which alone seemed to lack money, would immediately decrease if money were absolutely abolished everywhere.

To picture this more clearly, consider a barren and unfruitful year in which famine has taken away many thousand men. I firmly maintain that at the end of that shortage an examination of rich men's barns would reveal so much grain that, if it had been distributed among those killed by starvation, no one at all would have noticed the poor harvest. So easily could a living be made if that blessed thing money (a brilliant discovery to open up the way to a living) did not on its own shut off from us the path to a living. I am quite sure that the rich feel this too and are well aware how better a state it would be to lack nothing essential rather than abound in superfluities, to be taken from countless cares rather than be besieged by great wealth. Nor does it occur to me to doubt that the whole world could easily have been brought long ago to the laws of Utopia by the consideration of each man's advantage or by the authority of our Saviour Christ, who, with his great wisdom, could not fail to know what was best and, with his great kindness, could not fail to advise what he knew to be best. This would have been possible, if that single beast—the chief and parent of all plagues—pride did not fight against it. Pride measures her prosperity not by her own advantages, but by others' disadvantages. She would not even wish to become a goddess if there were no wretches left over whom she could rule and exult, by comparison with whose wretchedness her own felicity might shine, whose need she might torture and inflame by displaying her own riches. This serpent of hell creeping over the breasts of men drags them back and stops them from seeking a better way of life.

Since she is too deeply fixed in the hearts of men to be easily plucked out, I am glad that the Utopians at least have achieved this form of republic, though I greatly

wish all men had. The Utopians have followed those
rules of life with which they laid such foundations for
their republic as are most prosperous and also, as far as
the human mind may conjecture, destined to last forever.
For since they have cut out together with the other vices
the roots of ambition and strife, there is no danger of in-
ternal discord, which alone has destroyed the well protected riches of many cities. With their concord safe at
home and their institutions healthy, not even the jealousy
of all the neighboring princes could shake or move that
empire, although they have often tried in the past and
always been driven back.

So Raphael finished his account. Many points occurred to me where the ways and laws of that people
seemed regulated quite absurdly—for example, their
method of waging war, their religious practices and other
institutions of theirs too, but particularly the foundation
stone of the whole government—I mean their communal
life and living without any use for money, since by this
one enactment are overthrown all nobility, magnificence,
splendor and majesty, the true glory and ornaments, as
popular opinion goes, of a republic. Yet I knew he was
tired from his speech and I was not sure whether he could
tolerate any contrary opinion, especially as I remembered
he had censored others on that account, as if they were
afraid of being thought unintelligent if they could not
find something to criticize in others' discoveries. So I
praised the Utopians' constitution and Raphael's speech,
took him by the hand and led him indoors to dinner, saying that there would be another time for us to think more
deeply on those matters and discuss them more fully
with him. I hope this may happen someday. Meanwhile,

although I cannot agree with everything he said, although he is otherwise beyond all doubt a most learned man with deep experience of human affairs, yet I readily admit that in the republic of Utopia there are very many things that I would pray might come to our cities rather than hope they might ever be established.